Routledge Revivals

The Advanced Capitalist System

This book, first published in 1980, is based on a series of lectures entitled "Theoretical Problems of American Political Economy" that Lynn Turgeon made during the fall of 1978 at Moscow State University. *The Advanced Capitalist System: A Revisionist View* will be of interest to students of politics and economics.

The Advanced Capitalist System

A Revisionist View

Lynn Turgeon

Routledge
Taylor & Francis Group

First published in 1980
by M. E. Sharpe

This edition first published in 2015 by Routledge
2 Park Square, Milton Park, Abingdon, Oxon, OX14 4RN
and by Routledge
711 Third Avenue, New York, NY 10017

Routledge is an imprint of the Taylor & Francis Group, an informa business

© 1980 M. E. Sharpe, Inc.

Publisher's Note
The publisher has gone to great lengths to ensure the quality of this reprint but points out that some imperfections in the original copies may be apparent.

Disclaimer
The publisher has made every effort to trace copyright holders and welcomes correspondence from those they have been unable to contact.

A Library of Congress record exists under LC control number: 80051202

ISBN 13: 978-1-138-91929-7 (hbk)
ISBN 13: 978-1-315-68790-2 (ebk)

The
Advanced
Capitalist
System

A REVISIONIST VIEW

Lynn Turgeon

M. E. Sharpe, Inc.
White Plains, New York

Copyright © 1980 by M. E. Sharpe, Inc.
901 North Broadway, White Plains, N.Y. 10603

Library of Congress Cataloging in Publication Data

Turgeon, Lynn, 1920-
  The advanced capitalist system.

  Includes bibliographical references and indexes.
  1. Economic history—1945. 2. Inflation (Finance) and unemployment.
3. Capitalism. I. Title.
HC59.T86   330.12′2   80-51202
ISBN 0-87332-171-5
ISBN 0-87332-172-3 (pbk.)

Printed in the United States of America

Contents

Preface

In the fall of 1978 I was a Fulbright-Hays lecturer on "Theoretical Problems of American Political Economy" at Moscow State University. I resided in Moscow's Lenin Hills for three months. I was asked to plan one two-hour lecture each week, but the usual adjustment and scheduling problems, as well as the week that most Soviet citizens take off to celebrate the Revolution, meant that the series actually included only eight lectures. In addition, I lectured before the Political Economy *kafedra* (to which I was attached) early in the semester.

The subjects of my lectures were essentially the same ones discussed in my Economic Principles course at Hofstra University, and during the first meeting in the modern new Social Sciences Building—still under construction—I passed out the same class notes I use in the United States. Although I knew most of the students were comparatively advanced *aspiranty*, or graduate students, these notes were intended for any who might have a weak background in "bourgeois economics." As it turned out, many students were specialists studying various aspects of the capitalist system or the U.S. economy, and as a result of their broad backgrounds, the questioning was often sophisticated and critical.

As a long-time student of the Soviet system, I was able to illustrate some of the points made with examples from Soviet economic history. Wherever possible, I tried to couch my arguments to some extent in a Marxist framework and to provide examples more relevant to Soviet students. But, outside of this, I used essentially the same material and approach as at Hofstra.

Ordinarily I would meet my translator/interpreter the day before each class, at which time I would supply him with an advance copy of the lecture. If he had any questions as to the precise meaning of the text, we would iron them out before class. In no case was there ever any pressure put on me to change my text.

Although my Russian is not adequate to deliver an entire lecture, I was able to monitor and sometimes correct my translator. Since all the lectures and discussions were taped, I had an additional opportunity to review the translations. Ordinarily the first hour and a half would be devoted to the main text, with occasional pauses for impromptu discussion or supplementary material. This was followed by about thirty minutes of direct questions and answers. Despite the fact that the students knew that they were being taped, the discussions were scarcely inhibited.

As others have observed (Ed Ames, for example[1]), being away from one's own books and notes can be advantageous both in teaching and in writing. Despite some sacrifice of precision, what is presumably most important precipitates with an uncanny clarity. Having an entire week to prepare for a two-hour lecture was a luxury for someone used to a twelve-hour teaching load, and allowed for better organization. I did have the 1978 *Economic Report of the President*, and I subscribed to both the *Wall Stree Journal* and the *International Herald Tribune* to keep abreast of what was happening on the contemporary economic scene. The United States Embassy staff in Moscow—particularly the Fulbright supervisors, Barbara Allen and Pat Kushlis—was most cooperative in routing both the London *Economist* and *Business Week* my way.

The approach taken in my lectures is deliberately iconoclastic. And what better place to break a few icons than Soviet Russia? Soviet economists not surprisingly hold to some of the same myths about the U.S. economy that they read about in our conventional economics texts. Generally speaking, our Soviet counterparts assume that since military expenditures are a complete waste, the U.S. economy would be better off without such a burden. As we shall see, while this may be true for the USSR, it has hardly been so for us.

Soviet economists tend to agree with President Carter when he blames deficit financing for the inflation of the 1970s. Thus, they would go along with the President when he attempts to reduce wasteful government spending, particularly if it is related to the Defense Department. Like our monetarists, most (but not all) Soviet economists think of inflation as a monetary phenomenon, the result of too much money chasing too few goods—a situation that has been true in the Soviet Union. Thus, when I argued that the inflation of the 1970s was not caused by military spending, deficit financing, or too much money, I encountered a certain amount of disbelief, just as I do in the United States.

Soviet economists, like many economists on the left in the United States, also tend to believe that growing monopoly power and the resulting huge profits are causing the inflation of the 1970s. Thus, when they are confronted with the fact that profits as a percentage of total income have been weak since 1966, and that the service sector, which is relatively competitive, is the main engine of stagflation, they are as dumbfounded as their Western counterparts.

During the first session of my class, I attempted to outline the principal schools of thought within Western economics. Naturally, at the end of the lecture, one of the students wanted to know the school of thought to which I belonged. Rather than answer him directly, I suggested that the students listen throughout the semester. I promised to raise the same question during the last meeting, at which time I would give them an answer. The answer to this question is included here as Lecture X.

I should like to take this opportunity to thank my three Soviet *rukovoditeli*, or advisers, Georgi Tchibrikov (who sat in on all the lectures), Iskra Rudakova, and Sergei Tsarov. Dr. Tsarov, who was my translator-interpreter throughout, was indispensable. Dr. Marina Vcherashnaya, who translated some of my material into Russian so that I might read part of my lectures to the group, was particularly invaluable. Two American exchange students from the graduate program of the State University of New York at Albany, Bruce Drossman (my sound man) and Sam Middlebrooks (my editor), were also supportive in many ways. The latter also ferreted through the tapes of the lectures to reproduce the questions and answers at the end of the chapters. Finally, a special note of gratitude to Patricia Kolb for some helpful editorial suggestions.

NOTE

[1] Edward Ames, *Soviet Economic Processes* (Irwin, 1965), p. 9.

I.

Contemporary Schools of Economic Thought in the United States

During the postwar years, the study of economics in the United States has been dominated by Paul Samuelson's neoclassical synthesis. This synthesis was an attempt to integrate what we might refer to as Marshallian economics with the Keynesian model. In the wake of the "Keynesian Revolution," the role of the state would be to guarantee a full-employment framework within which Marshallian principles of economic rationality would again become relevant. The various state activities could also be subject to cost-benefit analysis, as discussed by my predecessor at Moscow State, Professor Earl Brubaker, last spring.

Paul Samuelson has frequently maintained that there is no such thing as Republican or Democratic economic theory. Richard Nixon claimed to be a Keynesian in 1971. Milton Friedman once argued that "we are all Keynesians now." And Arthur Okun proclaimed in 1969 the existence of a bipartisan consensus in economics. It is true that the Republicans and Democrats have both acted as if there were a negatively sloping Phillips curve and assumed that (1) increasing unemployment would control or reduce inflationary pressures; and (2) pushing back the economy toward full employment would exacerbate the inflation problem. But the parties put different priorities on the twin goals of creating full employment and controlling inflation. The Republicans are less interested in full employment and more interested in controlling inflation. This is to be expected, since they tend to represent the managerial class and can better bargain with labor if there is a reserve of unemployed workers. Besides, inflation tends to erode the value of their savings. The

Democrats, on the other hand, have put a higher priority on getting back to full employment (since one of their main supports comes from organized labor) and a lower priority on controlling inflation (since many of their constituents are debtors rather than lenders). As a consequence of this partisan difference we have a phenomenon that I have labeled "political business cycles."

Top economists, some of whom have been appointed to the Council of Economic Advisers, tend to operate within the bipartisan consensus. But they cover a whole range of views as to the proper weight to be given to the two major problems. Ranging from left to right, they might include: Walter Heller, James Tobin, William Nordhaus, Gardner Ackley, Arthur Okun, Paul McCracken, Henry Wallich, Henrik Houthakker, Herbert Stein, William Fellner, and at times, even Arthur Burns. We might say that this centrist group of economists is convinced that there is no need to change the historical proportions between investment and consumption, no need to adjust to lower returns to capital, and no need to move toward a more equal distribution of income. In fact, Arthur Okun feels that there is a certain trade-off between equality and efficiency. These economists thus tend to support still greater subsidies for investment, such as the investment tax credit. In effect, they subscribe to the paradigm of your prerevolutionary economist, Tugan-Baranowsky.[1]

In the seventies, this vital center of economics has come under attack from both sides of the political-economy spectrum. Fine tuning of the economy, using various combinations of monetary and fiscal policy and "leaning against the wind," has produced a condition referred to as stagflation. The past and present policies have tended to reduce the rate of economic growth, but the rate of inflation persists and even grows, contrary to the expectations of those believing that there is a negatively sloping Phillips curve. This crisis in mainstream economics has stimulated the emergence of economic dissenters, to whom we now turn.

Deviations to the left of the bipartisan consensus can be divided into three groups: the Institutionalists, the New Left, and the Old Left. The writings of the economists I have grouped as

Institutionalists can be found in the *Journal of Economic Issues*, published by the Association for Evolutionary Economics, and in the new *Journal of Post Keynesian Economics*.[2] New Left economists publish in the *Review of Radical Political Economics*, the organ of the Union for Radical Political Economics (URPE), and in *Monthly Review*. Old Left economists publish in *Political Affairs* and, to some extent, in *Science and Society*.

The Institutionalist group tends to put more weight on the problems of greater equality of income distribution. They may also put greater stress on cleaning up the environment and other social issues. John Kenneth Galbraith is probably the best example of this dissenting position, and on the basis of his most recent books could be classified as an evolutionary socialist. Certainly not all members of this group agree with all of Galbraith's rather extreme positions: *always* in the vanguard when it comes to price and wage controls; *never* in favor of cutting taxes; advocacy of a neutral monetary policy; and a certain admiration for the efficiency of the large corporation (as with Schumpeter, one of his intellectual ancestors, along with Veblen). Many members of this group subscribe to the statement of the Initiative Committee for National Economic Planning, which is one of the projects of Nobel prize-winner Wassily Leontief (the Russian father of input-output analysis, who teaches at New York University), labor leader Leonard Woodcock, and Myron Sharpe, Economist-Publisher of *Challenge* magazine.

Among the other well-known economists in this school are Robert Heilbroner, Robert Lekachman, Lester Thurow, Broadus Mitchell, Leon Keyserling, Alfred Eichner, Sidney Weintraub, and Martin Bronfenbrenner. Foreign economists operating within a similar paradigm include the group surrounding Joan Robinson and subscribing to Michal Kalecki's seminal works, as well as Piero Sraffa, Gunnar Myrdal, Jan Tinbergen, and Shigeto Tsuru.

Further to the left we find the New Left economists, a school that literally exploded out of the Vietnam War experience. They attempt to operate within a Marxist framework and reject a great deal of bourgeois economics. In contrast to the Old Left, they put great stress on decentralization of decision making and on having a small central bureaucracy. They tend to discount the importance of the division of labor and the need for greater efficiency generally, oppose nuclear power, stress the existing alienation of labor, and emphasize the negative side of the multinationals. An important book influencing their thinking is *Monopoly Capital* by Paul Sweezy and the late Paul Baran. Harry Magdoff's *Age of Imperialism* has also been influential.

Among the other economists in this school are Douglas Dowd, James O'Connor, David Gordon (who has recently taken an interest in your Kondratieff's long waves), William Tabb, Howard Sherman, E. K. Hunt, Dan Fusfeld, Ann Seidman, John Gurley, Richard Du Boff, Ray Franklin, David Mermelstein, Sam Bowles, Herb Gintis, Howard Wachtel, Anwar Shaikh, Arthur Mac Ewan, and Gar Alperovitz. In England, John Eatwell, Andrew Glyn, and Bob Sutcliffe seem to take about the same positions.

There is also an Old Left position, represented by the Communist Party, U.S.A. They tend to favor centralized planning, more or less resembling that of the USSR, and in this respect stand in contrast to the New Left, which has been relatively anti-Soviet and somewhat Maoist and Titoist. They are in favor of the development of nuclear power as an energy source, and have been opposed to the Equal Rights Amendment—which comes out of the women's movement and is therefore considered to be an upper- or middle-class demand. They are also in the vanguard when it comes to approving the expansion of East-West trade. Leading economists of this school are Victor Perlo, Ed Boorstein, and David Laibman.

There is also a right deviation, the so-called "Chicago School." This school of economists has never really accepted the Keynesian vision of the role of the state. They tend to assume that saving is necessary for investment activity to take place and that there is something of a capital shortage, and therefore they see a need for greater incentives to save. They vociferously proclaim that minimum-wage laws and generous unemployment compensation create unemployment above a "natural rate," and that free trade is necessarily a good thing for all concerned, something to be encouraged by floating exchange rates. If there are poor people, a negative income tax provision will solve any distribution problems.

Since 1964, at least, they have been in favor of cutting taxes, presumably with the object of reducing the role of government. At that time, Milton Friedman (who, according to speculation, was scheduled to be Chairman of Goldwater's Council of Economic Advisers) was advocating a series of tax cuts to be implemented over five consecutive years. More recently he has essentially supported Proposition 13 (a sharp limitation on property taxes) in California, and presumably sympathizes with Representative Kemp's bold tax-cut proposals.

There is some disagreement here over the proper role of the Federal Reserve Board. Most members of this school approve of the Board's conservative bias, but Friedman himself, à la Galbraith, would like to take the Board out of monetary-policy decision making altogether. (Otherwise, Friedman is usually on the opposite side of the fence from Galbraith.) Since this school of economists emphasizes the importance of saving, they see little harm coming from high interest rates or better returns to capital. One of their favorite platitudes is that "there is no such thing as a free lunch."

In addition to Friedman, there are his colleagues at Chicago, George Stigler, and his prize student, Gary Becker, one of the more innovative minds in bourgeois economics. Other "pre-Keynesians" include Alan Greenspan, William Simon, Warren Nutter, and many other economists who have come to believe that "money matters."

This school has had a recent success in California, where Proposition 13 carried by a large majority, and this ideology has spread rapidly throughout the country. It has the support of upper- and middle-class property owners, who happen to have high voter participation rates. Presumably the widespread cutting of taxes would generate a revitalization of the private sector and of capitalism generally.

What this movement fails to recognize is the fact that the growth of government under the advanced capitalist system is scarcely an accident. It is one of the stabilizers of the system, which—without the increasing role of the state—tends to have a falling rate of profit. The "paradox of thrift" also works with respect to government expenditures: saving or paring government expenditures does not guarantee that the private sector will fill the gap. It would, however, demonstrate that we have learned absolutely nothing from the experience of the Great Depression.

Theoretically, we should also have an "Old Right"—a conservative or authoritarian approach that stresses the need for a strong central government. Thus far, there seems to be no audience for these ideas discredited by Hitler. But should the extreme "Proposition 13 mentality" spread and lead to economic disaster, who can say that an old right position might not be resuscitated for the occasion? As Robert Heilbroner—in a recent *New Yorker* piece preparing his readers for an era of planning —says, there is still the question of who is to do the planning and in whose interest.[3]

Classical school of economics: Early economic philosophers— from Adam Smith through Karl Marx—who were principally interested in macroeconomic or development problems. They largely subscribed to a labor theory of value.

Neoclassical school of economics: Successors to the classical school of economics beginning in 1871 and including Jevons, Marshall, Irving Fisher, and Pigou. They were more interested in microeconomic problems, equilibrium pricing, and marginal utility as a determinant of value. They still assumed that Say's Law was valid and that crises or recessions were temporary deviations from the norm of full employment. The early Keynes (in *The Economic Consequences of the Peace* and the *Treatise on Money*) wrote in the neoclassical tradition. A quantity theory of money is assumed, with inflation caused primarily by too much money in the system. Policy proposals include cutting wages to restore full employment. These views are currently being expressed by Milton Friedman and can be labeled either as "New Right" or "pre-Keynesian."

Keynesian school of economics: Stems from Lord Keynes' *General Theory* (1936) and practiced by Germany and Japan in the 1930s, as well as by the United States during World War II and the postwar years until 1951. Leon Keyserling, Chairman of the Council of Economic Advisers under President Truman, who opposed the Treasury Accord of 1951, was the last major U.S. economist subscribing to this school of thought.

Post-Keynesian schools of economics: Until recently, this label was used to describe those economists believing in the neoclassical synthesis as expounded by Paul Samuelson. It involved a rebirth of the idea that monetary policy can be useful as part of the tool kit of the "fine tuners." It can also be referred to as the "bipartisan consensus," and includes the so-called "New Economists" of the Kennedy years—Heller, Tobin, and Ackley.

This same label is being used by the "neo-Keynesian" economists around Joan Robinson in Great Britain, and another small group of U.S. economists represented in a collection edited by Alfred S. Eichner, *A Guide to Post-Keynesian Economics*. They overlap to some extent with the Galbraithians, who can also be referred to as "Institutionalists," the intellectual descendents of Thorstein Veblen and John R. Commons. Both groups are inclined to expose the weaknesses of the theoretical underpinnings of conventional economic thought. Some members of this group are non-Marxist evolutionary socialists.

New Left school of economics: Constitutes a sharp break with bourgeois economics and goes back to Marx for its theoretical base. It emphasizes the need for decentralized decision making, is not impressed by the advantages of division of labor, and has been critical of Soviet central planning, but rather sympathetic to Chinese and Yugoslav experiments in planning.

Old Left school of economics: Holds that Soviet-type central planning, including increased reliance on nuclear power, is at least on the right track.

NOTES

[1] Michael Tugan-Baranowsky was a revisionist economist in the early twentieth century who denied the interdependence of production and consumption. According to Tugan-Baranowsky, production could expand indefinitely without regard to the level or trend in consumption. See Paul Sweezy, *The Theory of Capitalist Development*, Oxford, 1942, pp. 158 *et seq*.

[2] The title of the Post Keynesian group's new journal is somewhat confusing since Paul Samuelson and others have called the bipartisan consensus "Post-Keynesian" for some time. To distinguish themselves from the Samuelsonian school, as well as from the Robinsonians of Great Britain, the journal's editors dropped the hyphen in Post Keynesian.

[3] The long *New Yorker* article has appeared in book form: Robert Heilbroner, *Beyond Boom and Crash*, Norton, 1978, reviewed by Bernard D. Nossiter in the *International Herald Tribune*, October 24, 1978, p. 14. For my review of this book, see *In These Times*, January 16-22, 1980, p. 17.

II.

Defense and Military Expenditures

For a long time the role of defense expenditures was simply ig-
nored by most economists in the United States. Such spending
was considered to be something of an anomaly and certainly exogenous to the system. If only the Russians and their system
didn't exist, we could stop wasting resources and go about our
traditional economic business of economizing on scarce resources. Most conventional texts had one or two references to
military spending, since it was rather difficult to talk about the
Federal budget without at least mentioning the fact that from
one-third to one-half of these expenditures were for military
purposes.

   Two events broke this silence. One was Premier Khrushchev's visit to the United States in 1959 and his talk before the
Economics Club in New York City. Khrushchev, who at the
time was propagandizing for peaceful coexistence—the fore-
runner of détente—ventured his optimistic opinion that there
was no economic reason why the United States couldn't seriously
consider the disarmament proposals that were then being initiated by the Soviet Union. Up until this point, the conventional
Marxist and Soviet view had been less optimistic. The other
event was President Eisenhower's farewell address to the nation
in January 1961, warning the American people about the dan-
gers of a "military-industrial complex," a term that has since become part of our standard vocabulary. This was particularly appropriate since the Republicans (led by Richard Nixon) had recently lost a close election in which the military sided with the
Democrats (led by John F. Kennedy) in their charge that Eisen-

hower's eight-year $40 billion lid on defense spending had produced a "missile gap."

The experts came to believe that—with a proper expansion of the economy using easier monetary and fiscal policies—defense expenditures might be reduced. Work by such economists as Professor William Vickrey of Columbia University reinforced this position. This view was also supported by the writings of Charles Hitch, then of the RAND Corporation, who claimed that profits were even lower in defense than in nondefense sectors. Later, this same general position led to the expectation that there would be some sort of "peace dividend" after the Vietnam War.

The traditional view of military spending also shows up in the bipartisan analysis of the economic effects of the Vietnam War. In the view of Samuelson and others, the effect of the Vietnam War was similar to that of earlier mobilizations—World Wars I and II and the Korean conflict. The war was supposedly fought at full employment with demand-pull inflation bidding resources away from the civilian sector. If only we had raised taxes in 1966 instead of two years later, in July 1968, we would have been able to finance the war without the demand-pull inflation that eventually accelerated.

International comparisons appear to reinforce this traditional position. When one looks at the Japanese and West German economies in the postwar years, it is possible to explain their rapid growth and respective "economic miracles" by the comparatively low defense budgets that had been imposed by the occupying powers. This was particularly true for Japan, where the defense budget in the postwar years has traditionally accounted for no more than 1 percent of gross national product. But the West Germans too, with 3 to 4 percent of their gross national product going to the military sector, have been on the low side in comparison to Great Britain. The latter country has had a particularly sluggish stop-and-go economy, produced in part by high defense expenditures. Britain's leaders, in a desperate attempt to preserve the British Empire, began to allocate around 7 percent of their gross national product to defense almost immediately after World War II.

All the above analyses remind one of an intellectual "Potemkin Village." Rather than being exogenous to the system, U.S. military spending appears to have endogenous origins. In particular, there seems to be a relationship between changes in defense expenditures and the political party in the White House. In the postwar years, the Democrats have been associated with increases in defense spending, while the Republicans—with the possible exception of President Ford—have tended to stabilize or even reduce military spending.

The result has been the development of what I have already referred to as political business cycles. Eight years of Democratic military expansion or stimulation has been followed by eight years of Republican relaxation. As a result, profits have tended to be higher, economic expansion more vigorous, and unemployment lower under the Democrats than under the Republicans. We now seem to have embarked on our third Democratic expansion of military spending.[1]

Among the fifty states there has been considerable variation in the amount of economic activity emanating from the national defense budget. In general, there is a positive relationship between the amount of defense spending and relative growth, despite the conscious policy of the Pentagon to award contracts to regions having higher unemployment rates.[2] This dependence on military activity is particularly evident whenever a military decision is made to close a redundant base. The outcries from the local inhabitants dependent on this activity for their livelihood are echoed in the outraged speeches of their representatives and senators in the halls of Congress.

The claim that profits are lower in defense than in nondefense industries is based on a relatively meaningless comparison of profits as a percentage of sales in the two sectors. Since the defense sector is subject to considerably more prime contracting and subcontracting, the large defense contractors (such as Boeing) are pretty much like large retail food distributors, who simply assemble the final product of a myriad of subcontractors. Naturally, since the value added of all the subcontractors is included in the final sales figure, profits as a percentage of sales for the prime contractors look remarkably low, just as they do for the supermarket chains.

A more meaningful comparison of profits—such as profits as a percentage of capital invested or profits as a percentage of value added—indicates that they are higher in defense than they are in nondefense. This was the unmistakable conclusion of a detailed study conducted by the General Accounting Office and publicized by Senator William Proxmire several years ago. Some attempt has been made to justify these higher profits by the supposedly higher risk involved in such a business, but the assumed risk of disarmament seems minimal.

The claim that the Vietnam War was a typical war in which we had full employment and demand-pull inflation simply doesn't hold much water. It was a war during which we not only had an important mini-recession (1966-67), but also a full-fledged recession (1969-71). The chief evidence for the claim that the war created full employment lies in the unemployment rate of labor in 1968 and early 1969. The problem here is that a great deal of the true slack in the labor market was concealed by extensive manpower retraining programs left over from President Johnson's "Great Society" programs.[3]

When we look at the capital unemployment rate—especially before the Federal Reserve Board managed to revise the data—we see a pretty continuous decline in the rate of utilization for our capital plant and equipment after 1966. The sluggishness of profits and labor productivity during the whole period after 1966 is also uncharacteristic of conditions during a period of full employment and demand-pull inflation, such as the Korean conflict years.

The mini-recession is a particularly interesting experience that deserves more serious examination. For almost a year—the second half of 1966 and the first half of 1967—insignificant growth occurred despite the sharp increase in defense expenditures connected with the escalation of the Vietnam War. The economy actually declined in the first quarter of 1967 and barely increased in the second quarter of the year, thus giving rise to the term "mini-recession." A full-fledged recession, according to the National Bureau of Economic Research, must have two consecutive quarters during which real gross national product declines.

The strange slowdown in the economy associated with the surge in military spending caused at least one business economist (Eliot Janeway) to proclaim in a book that wars were no longer functional for the advanced capitalist system.[4] Wall Street, which was greatly influenced by this book and the newsletter published by its author, abruptly reversed itself with respect to the Vietnam War. Before 1967, peace feelers by the Vietcong tended to depress stock prices, while afterwards, they tended to have a bullish effect.

In my view, the mini-recession was brought about by a combination of much too tight monetary and fiscal policy. The tightness of monetary policy stems back to December 1965, when the Federal Reserve Board jumped the gun and began to tighten credit prematurely. This ultimately led to what was later called the "credit crunch." Despite President Johnson's appeal to the Board's Chairman, William McChesney Martin, the higher interest rates stuck and by mid-1966 had brought housing construction to a near standstill. On the fiscal side, the government suspended for four months the tax credit for investments, which had stimulated the investment binge that began in 1962. The withholding of income taxes was made progressive at this time, resulting in a significant increase in current tax revenues and thereby tending to brake the war-generated expansion.

By 1967, it had become clear that the fine tuners had gone too far, and the investment tax credit was reinstated with embarrassment. But it seems obvious that if tax rates had been increased still more in 1966—we would have had at least a medi-recession rather than a mini-one.

The evaporation of any fiscal peace dividend after the conclusion of the Vietnam War also raises doubts about the conventional view. When the war expenditures began to taper off in 1970, the economy also began to slow down. As a result, we were saddled with a huge passive deficit (roughly $90 billion during the first Nixon term) rather than any fiscal surplus or dividend. President Nixon himself tended to explain his first recession of 1969-71 precisely in terms of his reductions in military spending. This is not to say that a certain combination of aggressively bold monetary and fiscal policy might not have engineered a fiscal dividend, but rather that the bipartisan consensus, guiding Okun and McCracken alike, was incapable of producing it.

Some researchers on the left, and notably those whose

work has been financed by the Machinists' Union, stress the fact that more jobs can be created per million dollars spent on the programs of nondefense government agencies (housing, education, etc.) than on military spending. Their argument resembles that advanced by development economists for the Third World when they argue that labor-intensive projects are preferable to the capital-intensive ones typically introduced by multinational corporations.

These calculations simply reflect the fact that value added per worker is higher in defense than it is in nondefense government expenditures. Thus wages, productivity, and profits— hardly an insignificant factor—would also seem to be higher in defense than in nondefense activity.

As in the case of underdeveloped countries, the object of national economic policy in the advanced capitalist world should be to reduce jobs *per se* via the substitution of capital for labor, provided full employment is achieved through successful implementation of fiscal policy. For, as Adam Smith saw clearly, work is ultimately only a means to a rational end—the consumption of useful goods and services. Otherwise, we find ourselves advancing "leaf-raking" or other featherbedding projects because more jobs can be created in this process than by other means. The same argument can be illogically made for a return to a labor-intensive draft rather than a voluntary army, and it is no coincidence that the Carter Administration has been hinting at a possible return to this inefficient employment-creating institution.[5]

It is important to explain the relationship between defense expenditures and the postwar prosperity or lack thereof in the advanced capitalist countries. We should recall that two broad types of economies existed after the war: those that had little or no capital destruction—the United States and Canada—and those that had to begin capital construction anew—particularly Japan, West Germany, and Great Britain. Japan and West Germany were also unique in that they had to absorb roughly six million of their own nationals, who were repatriated as a result of postwar agreements.

In effect, this huge influx of labor and terrible capital destruction had recreated nineteenth-century capitalist conditions —a capital shortage, a labor surplus, and a deliberately imposed free-market economy that produced impressive results in the short run. The very high rates of profit in these years were an important attraction for U.S. multinational corporations, which were enthusiastically expanding their overseas activities.

Canada is a particularly interesting example since the Canadian economy remained intact and was much less affected by the military build-up over Korea and the Cold War generally. Canada was also unique in that it experimented with a floating exchange rate during most of the 1950s while other countries were following International Monetary Fund principles of fixed exchange rates with occasional devaluations. The result was the poorest economic record of all the advanced capitalist countries in the late fifties. Only after the Canadian dollar was fixed in relationship to other currencies and devalued in 1961, and the Canadians began to trade with the noncapitalist world on a large scale, did prosperity and vigorous postwar growth take place in that country.

Great Britain, which had a great deal of capital destroyed during World War II, attempted to maintain the myth that it was still a great imperial power after the war. Britain's initial recovery was financed by a huge loan from the United States at 2 percent interest and the forgiving of Lend-Lease debts. The price of this largess was a special relationship between the United States and Great Britain. In this manner the United States encouraged the British to maintain a military budget that was far higher than needed and cut into any proper modernization of their plant and equipment.

Thus, while one can say that defense spending played a negative role in countries such as Great Britain that had great capital destruction, the same cannot be said either for the United States or Canada. It seems rather safe to assume that the United States enjoyed postwar prosperity *because* of the cold-war expenditures —including the Marshall Plan—rather than *despite* them. These one-way movements of goods created employment and profits at home and averted the postwar recession that almost all Keynesians had anticipated.

It is also highly significant that Japanese military expenditures have been rising recently by about tenfold and now amount to some $15 billion yearly.[6] One might think that the slowdown in the Japanese economy since 1973 is somehow related to these increased defense expenditures. But in this connection we must distinguish between cause and effect. I would argue that the slowdown produced the tendency to develop military spending as a stabilizer (on the down side), as has been the case in the United States. At any rate, there doesn't seem to be any exogenous factor (outside of U.S. encouragement) that could account for this sharp increase in Japanese defense expenditures. The West German military budgets likewise tended to rise as sluggishness developed after 1973, but that country has also relied on trade with Eastern Europe to create some half million jobs. In this respect, the Japanese were at a disadvantage as long as the Maoist principle of "balanced equivalents" prevailed in the People's Republic of China.

One of the most ardent critics of military spending in the United States has been Victor Perlo of the Old Left. Since 1959 he has attempted to play up the role of defense spending as a "destabilizer" and as a generator of inflation. In the *Daily World*, July 6, 1978, he argued that "the arms race is the central dynamic force behind inflation." According to Perlo, the "declining share of GNP [accounted for by defense] is a misleading calculation." He feels that "it's quite accurate to say that if military spending had been kept at the already exorbitant level of 1973, and other budget items left as they are, there would be no federal deficit today."[7]

The problem with this position is that it doesn't give President Nixon proper credit for reducing real defense expenditures, as can be seen in the table on p. 17. It is highly significant, in my view, that the greatest recent increases in the price level have taken place during the years when real defense outlays were declining. Perlo's analysis also fails to distinguish between "active" and "passive" deficits, which will be dealt with in the following chapter.

Startling as it may sound, the deficits of the 1970s are not so much brought about by increased government spending as they are by the lack of government spending. In other words, they come from inadequate tax revenues because of unemployed re-

Nominal and Real Defense Spending, United States, 1968-77

Years	National Defense (billion current dollars)	Implicit GNP Price Deflator (1972 = 100)	Real Defense Spending (billion 1972 dollars)	Real GNP (1972 Dollars)	Column 4 as % of Column 5
(1)	(2)	(3)	(4)	(5)	(6)
1968	76.9	82.57	93.1	1,051.8	8.9
1969	76.3	86.72	88.0	1,078.8	8.2
1970	73.5	91.36	80.4	1,075.3	7.5
1971	70.2	96.02	73.1	1,107.5	6.6
1972	73.5	100.00	73.5	1,171.1	6.3
1973	73.5	105.80	69.4	1,235.0	5.6
1974	77.0	116.02	66.4	1,217.8	5.5
1975	83.9	127.18	66.0	1,202.3	5.5
1976	86.8	133.88	64.8	1,271.0	5.1
1977 (preliminary)	94.3	141.32	66.7	1,332.7	5.0
1977 (preliminary last quarter)	98.6	141.32	70.0	1,354.5	5.2

Source: *Economic Report of the President*, 1978, pp. 257, 262.

sources. It might be possible to argue that military spending has prevented deflation in the postwar years, but it doesn't seem to be the chief culprit behind cost-push inflation. While one can appreciate the political motivations behind Perlo's analysis, it is still either pre-Keynesian or post-Keynesian in its premises.

In my view, military expenditures represent an important stabilizer and serve as a prop for the declining rate of profit. The fact that so much research and development has been funded by Congress through appropriations to military and space budgets should not be overlooked either. The recent decline in these expenditures, which Walt W. Rostow so deplores,[8] seems somehow related to the overall sluggishness of the leading member of the advanced capitalist system.

Q. *What is the role of military expenditures, and is there a contradiction between the growth of military expenditures and détente?*

A. President Carter really needs to decide between a continuation of détente or increased military spending. Up until now he has been rather uncertain about which road to take. It is quite clear that he can't take both roads indefinitely. You might want to look at my paper, "How Much Longer Can the Carter Expansion Continue?" which was passed out last time. Which way is he going to stimulate the economy? Nixon made a decision for détente and rejected defense spending as a stimulant to growth. During his 1970-71 recession, Nixon acknowledged the fact that reduced real defense spending was creating his first recession. The question is: can Carter undo what Nixon began? It's something of a trade-off. It's a little bit like a Phillips curve, negatively sloping, with increased military spending and détente on the two axes. East-West trade has the same effect as military spending. We have been exporting to the USSR six times more than we have been importing.

Q. *Can you transfer resources from the military sector to the energy sector?*

A. There is Walt Rostow's idea (*Getting From Here to There*) of government investment in energy. It would be a clever way to handle the transition problem——one that has potentialities. But the energy industry is really opposed to government planning. The problem is one of convincing the oil companies that you have to have federal investment in energy. The oil companies own some of the coal companies and the nuclear power plants as well. In general, the large corporation doesn't realize its inadequacy in solving this problem. There is also another problem. High OPEC prices have stimulated the discovery of additional oil such as in Mexico, so that it's difficult to convince the American people that there is a shortage requiring special measures. There is actually a surplus of oil on the west coast, since Alaskan oil has begun to flow to this area.

Q. *If the Soviet Union reduces its defense spending and satisfies its domestic consumers, won't it also have a realization problem?*

A. I would argue that the Soviet system will never have a realization problem. In fact, I wrote a book arguing this position, and you can find it in the Akademiia Nauk Social Science Library at Profsoiuznyi metro stop (*The Contrasting Economies*, Allyn and Bacon, 2nd edition, 1969). My students ask me this same question, which is one reason I wrote this book. The two economies are very different. The reason why you will never have a realization problem is that you have socialized what you might call surplus value. Nobody has a vested interest in the margin between the price level and the cost level. So that margin can be reduced over time through the planning process without ever developing a realization problem. In our system, individuals have an interest of a personal nature in profits, interest, dividends, and rent, and all of these are related to the investment process. If the rate of profit falls, the rate of private investment falls, requiring more and more government intervention in the market. Up until now the intervention has frequently been military spending. We already have a tremendous surplus capacity in relationship to all of the people who would like to use it and who are able to "vote" through their spending power. In other words, our income distribution is relatively fixed so that the people who still have the needs do not have the income to make the capacity work efficiently. To remedy this, there has to be a fundamental redistribution of income, to put spending power into the hands of poorer people. In your type of system, the income distribution is a planning decision. In order to avoid the production gap, you have to have a gradual equalization of income over time. In other words, our income distribution is inadequate for the full utilization of our resources. This will be dealt with in the final lecture on our schedule.

Q. *How does military spending solve this problem?*

A. It can solve it in the sense that you certify consumers through military spending. In fact, all of our waste institutions are the result of the failure to move toward greater equality. If the market forces do not produce enough consumers, then the military sector produces them through employment in the Defense Department or in the factories producing military hardware.

Q. *You say that East-West trade can accomplish the same thing as the expansion of military spending. Then why is it that so many businessmen and economists in the United States are against the expansion of East-West trade with the Soviet Union?*

A. As I see it, the large capitalists recognize the functional nature of East-West trade. If you look at who is in the vanguard, it is the large capitalists. Paradoxically, one of the main oppositions to East-West trade is organized labor. Some of the most progressive thinking is found among the large industrial capitalists. Notice that I say "industrial" capitalists, because there is a difference between them and the financial capitalists. One of the reasons why organized labor is so opposed to East-West trade is because one of the chief advisers to George Meany is a man named Jay Lovestone, a former Communist, who is very antagonistic toward communism now.

Q. *Is there a problem about the servicing of the debt by the socialist countries? There is a lot of talk in the West about the fact that the East European countries are too much in debt, that the export surplus is financed by debt.*

A. It is true that the debt to the West has risen, particularly in Poland and Hungary. But, in general, Eastern European countries borrow at preferential interest rates. [*N.B.* More recently, both Poland and Hungary have been forced to negotiate loans at premium interest rates.—L.T.] In an era of inflation, this borrowing looks like a good deal for the CMEA countries. In the case of the USSR, the high speculators' price for gold has helped reduce the relative size of their debt. And presumably, Soviet gold could be used ultimately to prevent any default on East European debt.

NOTES

[1] Although military spending took off again after President Carter assumed office, he did make two military decisions that were unpopular within the United States—stopping the B-1 bomber and postponing the neutron bomb. Carter could also claim that the total appropriated was 2 percent less than that projected by President Ford.

[2] Since there is a lag before the effect of the military spending can take place in the depressed area, the positive correlation persists. See Murray L. Weidenbaum and Ben-Chuh Liu, "Effects of Disarmament on Regional Income Distribution," *Journal of Peace Research*, no. 1, 1966, p. 90.

[3] At one point, almost one million persons were employed in administering, training, and being trained in these programs. When no jobs were available at the end of the training period, the trainees simply signed up for additional training programs.

[4] Eliot Janeway, *The Economics of Crisis: War, Politics and the Dollar*, Weybright and Talley, 1968.

[5] See my "Compulsory Military Service is Bad Economics," *The Hofstra Review*, Spring 1968, pp. 1-4.

[6] Henry Scott-Stokes, "Japan Would Like to Help, But . . . ," *New York Times*, April 29, 1979, p. E3.

[7] *Daily World*, September 14, 1978.

[8] Walt W. Rostow, *Getting From Here to There*, McGraw-Hill, New York, 1978, Chapter IX.

III.

Government Budgets, Deficit Financing, Lending and Granting

Before World War II, the role of government budgets and deficits had tended to increase during wartime and contract during the postwar years. As a result, it could be said that the greater share of our national debt was a consequence of wartime deficit financing under demand-pull inflationary conditions. Thus, it has been generally assumed that deficit financing—particularly if the lender of last resort is the central banking system—is inflationary. By the same token, it has also been assumed that all military spending is automatically inflationary.

If a country fought a war and ended up on the losing side, not only would it end up with a domestic deficit, but it would frequently be forced to pay reparations to the victor. Thus, at the conclusion of the Franco-Prussian War of 1871, a large indemnity was imposed on the vanquished country, France. In the early 1870s, the fact that postwar France was enjoying great prosperity while paying reparations to the victor puzzled economists. Still more paradoxical, the postwar German economy was concomitantly depressed although the Germans were receiving French reparations payments.

After World War I the young John Maynard Keynes made a great reputation as a result of his *Economic Consequences of the Peace*, written as a critique of the Versailles Treaty—in the framing of which he took part. The main thrust of Keynes' critique was that the $30 billion in reparations imposed upon the loser, Germany, was too heavy a burden. According to Keynes, the postwar German nation, which was shorn of a certain amount of its prewar productive capacity, would never be able to produce the goods necessary for the reparations payments imposed by the Treaty.

During World War I the United States lent large sums of money to various Allies, especially England and France, to assist them in prosecuting the war against Germany. After the war both countries insisted on receiving German reparations which were supposedly necessary to permit them to pay off their obligations to the United States. But, as the noneconomist John Foster Dulles wisely suggested (in a speech at the Commodore Hotel in New York City in March 1921), the main postwar problem would be the eventual inability of the U.S. economy to absorb the goods which the postwar German reparations and the subsequent British and French debt-repayment required.

A temporary solution was found in the Dawes Plan of 1924, under which the United States could lend large sums of money to postwar Germany to allow the losers to at least go through the motions of paying reparations. When the time came for repayment of these loans, or an extension of new loans, the world was headed into the Great Depression. President Hoover eventually solved this problem in 1931 by proposing a "moratorium" —which in fact meant that the war debts were to be permanently written off the books.

As a result of the new economic thinking after the appearance of Keynes' *The General Theory* in 1936, the debts and reparations after World War II were handled more smoothly in the interests of preserving and strengthening the system. The chief intellectual interpreters for postwar policy-makers were Etienne Mantoux (*The Carthaginian Peace; or, The Economic Consequences of Mr. Keynes*) and Jacob Viner writing in *Foreign Affairs* in 1943. Mantoux, using the Keynesian paradigm of 1936, was able to mount a devastating critique of the early Keynes' interpretation of the Versailles Treaty. Using Keynesian hindsight, it is possible to say that if the Germans had been permitted to pay the reparations of the Versailles Treaty over many years, this could have been an important employment-creating institution preventing the rise of Hitler. Keynes himself, when pressed by friends to develop a post—World War II reparations policy, referred to the whole problem as hopeless. But this was before the Cold War appeared on the scene to solve the dilemma.

As a result of Stalin's prodding, Roosevelt agreed at Yalta that roughly $10 billion could be taken out of the postwar German economy, a figure that was later confirmed by Truman at Potsdam. While Secretary of State Jimmy Byrnes was willing to permit the USSR to extract reparations from what is now the German Democratic Republic, the United States, as a result of the experience of the twenties, made no serious effort to extract reparations from either the West Germans or the Japanese. On the contrary, the Marshall Plan eventually meant that the victor (the United States) was in effect paying nearly $15 billion in reparations to Western Europe, including the defeated Germans.

The British, whose economy (unlike that of the United States) was indeed damaged by the Germans and might conceivably have benefited from reparations, were pacified by the postwar $3.63 billion British loan referred to in the last chapter, as well as the writing off of their lend-lease obligations.

Eventually, after their economies more or less recovered from the devastation of the war, both Japan and West Germany paid reparations to less-developed countries—various Asian countries (excluding China) in the case of Japan, and to Jews living in Israel in the case of the West Germans. The Japanese reparations payments continued well into the seventies, gradually providing jobs and profits for Japanese industry.

At the end of the Vietnam War, Secretary of State Henry Kissinger promised the victorious Vietnamese roughly $3 billion in reparations, but a recalcitrant Congress has as yet refused to fulfill this obligation.

We can now make a number of generalizations with respect to war reparations on the basis of recent economic history. An advanced capitalist country that has no capital destruction should avoid receiving reparations and if possible should make restitution or reparations to the war-damaged loser, which at the time should be able to absorb the required shipments of goods. As soon as recovery is assured, the loser can then create employment and make profits out of paying reparations to less-developed countries, which are ordinarily eager to import capital goods.

The same basic principle applies to debts generally. The advanced capitalist system, which tends to have a surplus of idle capital at existing rates of profit, is ordinarily very anxious to make loans or to extend—either in loans at preferential rates of interest or in outright grants—foreign aid, a postwar Keynesian employment-creating institution. At the same time, if the loans cannot be paid back there is little reluctance to refinance or even cancel the obligation. The recent decisions of Sweden, Canada, Great Britain, the Netherlands, Norway, and West Germany to cancel the obligations of the thirty poorest countries in the so-called "Fourth World" are consistent with this principle.[1]

The principles underlying United States Public Law 480 illustrate this clearly. In the postwar years, the principal problem facing agricultural policy makers in the United States was the disposal of the surplus that our highly productive agricultural sector made possible. Generally speaking, productivity has been growing at a much faster rate in agriculture than it has in the industrial sector of the U.S. economy.

Since U.S. taxpayers—particularly those from minority groups—would find outright gifts of the surplus food unpalatable, it was decided that the food shipments should be in the form of sales repayable in nonconvertible foreign currencies. In other words, the proceeds would somehow have to be spent on the spot. In this way there would never be any problem for the United States to accept goods from underdeveloped countries as payment.

A few college professors, diplomats, or U.S. businessmen abroad could have access to these U.S. foreign currency holdings, but in general they simply piled up or accumulated in the countries receiving the surplus food. Occasionally they might be released in an area suffering from an earthquake (as, for example, in Skopje, Yugoslavia), but in the main they proved to be unspendable. Thus, when Senator Patrick Moynihan became Ambassador to India one of his first acts was to write off about $2 billion worth of these Indian obligations.

Since World War II there has been a considerable growth of the national debt in the United States, in contrast to the earlier postwar experiences, when the role of government and deficit financing contracted. Even during the New Deal the deficit financing was minimal in comparison with the postwar years, since it was then believed that there was something fiscally irresponsible about paying out more than the Treasury took in. One of the important causes of the 1937-38 downturn in the economy was apparently a sharp reduction in deficit financing, with the result that there was still double-digit unemployment prior to the entry of the United States into the war.

Looking back on the experiences of both Germany and Japan before World War II, we can see a much more aggressive application of Keynesian principles, which resulted in full employment for Germany by 1936, and even earlier for Japan. Is it surprising that the increase in the national debt required to bring this about was less than pre-Keynesian economists expected? Using our present terminology, we can say that this is the first example of "active" deficit financing producing comparatively small increases in the national debt.

Up until the early sixties, the U.S. national debt was still less than it had been at the end of World War II. Since our gross national product had grown rapidly during this period, the debt as a percentage of gross national product had fallen dramatically, as can be seen in the table. More recently, however, particularly after 1970, the federal debt has grown rapidly, more or less keeping pace with the growth of gross national product. At the

National Debt as Percent of Gross National Product, U.S.A., Selected Years

Year	Gross National Product (billions current dollars)	Federal Debt* (billions current dollars)	Column 3 as % of Column 2
(1)	(2)	(3)	(4)
1945	212.3	252.5	119
1950	286.2	217.4	76
1955	399.3	229.6	58
1960	506.0	239.8	47
1965	688.1	266.4	39
1970	982.4	301.1	31
1975	1528.8	446.3	29
1976	1706.5	515.8	30
1977	1890.4	536.2	28

Source: *Economic Report of the President*, 1978, pp. 257, 337.

present it is hovering around 30 percent of gross national product.

As long as deflation can be avoided, we can agree with the post-Keynesians that there should be no serious problem coming out of the increase in the national debt. If real interest rates were actually being paid on this debt we might have a factor contributing to greater inequality in the distribution of income, but in general, the rate of inflation has exceeded the nominal interest payments on the debt.

Until 1962, American presidents continued to pay lip service to the importance of presenting a balanced budget to Congress. The fulfillment of the budget was something else, however. This was particularly true whenever there was a recession, as in 1958, when the declines in government revenues due to unemployed labor and capital produced a $13 billion deficit— what we can now refer to as a "passive deficit." Paradoxically, the Korean War produced a comparatively insignificant increase in the national debt due to the reemployment of underutilized resources inherited from the 1949 recession. In the first year of the war there was in fact a $6 billion surplus in the budget.

President Kennedy's Yale University speech in 1962 thus broke new ground. In this speech Kennedy indicated that the "New Economics" (as propounded by Heller, Tobin, and Ackley) did not require the submission of an annually balanced budget. Rather, he declared that the budget should be used as an instrument in the fine-tuning process, with deficits in times when resources were underutilized, and surpluses when it was time to cool off an "overheated economy."

In the early sixties American policy makers worried about the sluggishness in the growth rate inherited from the Eisenhower years. This was also the period when Premier Khrushchev boasted that the Soviet economy would eventually overtake the advanced capitalist system and "competitive coexistence" was in the air. As a consequence, the Kennedy "New Economists" began to develop the concept of the production gap. This calculation estimated what the economy would look like if there were full employment and measured the distance between the actual output and the capacity output. The object of economic policy then became one of closing or reducing the existing production gap.

At about the same time, the New Economists began to look at what the government budget would look like if there were full employment. They concluded that presently unemployed resources would begin paying taxes rather than require transfer payments—welfare or unemployment compensation. This calculation was then referred to as the "full-employment balance." In the early sixties it was estimated that the full-employment balance would show a surplus of some magnitude, which was then labeled "fiscal drag." According to the New Economists, existing tax rates were too high and causing a premature braking of the economy before full employment could be achieved.

The prescription for fiscal drag was a cutting of tax rates. It was comparatively easy for President Kennedy to cut business taxes as he did via the new investment tax credit and increases in rapid depreciation allowances, both of which occurred in 1962. But at the time of his assassination in November 1963, Congress was clearly still opposed to his planned reduction in personal income taxes. Shortly thereafter, however, President Johnson was able to engineer the passage of both a cut in personal taxes and large appropriations for a "War on Poverty" through a contrite Congress.

As a result of the tax cuts fiscal drag was reduced, and the economy very nearly got back to full employment in 1966. Miraculously, the tax revenues collected began to increase rapidly, so that the budget deficit very nearly disappeared. Washington jokesters proclaimed that the way to raise revenue was to lower taxes. Today a group of radical Republicans is attempting to profit from this experience by advocating sharp tax cuts, as provided by the Kemp-Roth bill.

Some of the New Economists in their euphoria began to talk about the expected appearance of a surplus at full employment, which they labeled the "fiscal dividend." According to their writings, the principal future problem would be for the government to come up with new ways to spend this dividend. The New Economists had seemingly managed to bring about elimination of business cycles, and the longest uninterrupted expansion of the economy continued, albeit with a relatively mild mini-recession in early 1967.

The amount of deficit-financing during the early part of the Vietnam War was surprisingly small and due in part to the passive deficit associated with the mini-recession. Congress finally approved the 10 percent income-tax surcharge, in response to the persistent demands of the bipartisan consensus, in July 1968. This measure produced our last small federal surplus in fiscal 1969. President Nixon soon eliminated the surcharge to cushion his first recession, and the total increase in the national debt during his first term amounted to around $90 billion.

But it is important to realize that this increase in deficit financing was largely passive, the result of underutilized resources which couldn't pay taxes and which required increased welfare spending. By the mid-seventies it was argued that for every one percentage point reduction in the unemployment rate, net government revenues would rise by $18 billion ($16 billion in increased tax revenues and $2 billion in reduced welfare spending).

Another characteristic of the Nixon years, in addition to the large passive deficits, was a sharp increase in revenue sharing. In his desire to reduce the powers of the federal government, President Nixon developed programs that would allow state and local governments discretionary power over the spending of federal tax revenues. Thus, to the extent that the state and local governments failed to increase their spending, large surpluses began to accumulate in certain state and local government budgets (which eventually led to Proposition 13 in California's election in June 1978). This was particularly true in energy-producing states after the OPEC agreement produced oases of prosperity resulting from higher energy prices. Today the aggregate surpluses at the state and local government level are exceeding $30 billion yearly, and 45 states are showing surpluses.

If we calculate the full employment balance for all levels of government, we would probably find today that there is considerable fiscal drag preventing the attainment of full employment, much as in 1962. The 1978 *Economic Report of the President* estimates a federal high-employment deficit of $18 billion, while the high-employment surplus at the state and local government levels would amount to $42.5 billion producing a net fiscal drag of about $25 billion.[2]

The calculation of the full-employment balance has become something of a political issue since the resulting balance depends on how full employment is defined. The higher the "full-employment unemployment rate," the lower the fiscal drag. Presumably, monetarists might define a full-employment unemployment rate of 6 percent and find that we are now running a deficit at full employment. On the other hand, if we assume a full-employment unemployment rate of 4 percent—as in the Humphrey-Hawkins bill—we would find a surplus at full employment. In the first case, we might prescribe a tax increase, while in the latter case, a tax reduction is called for.

It should be understood that there are three possible results when the full-employment balance is calculated. The full-employment budget can be balanced, in deficit, or show a surplus. When President Nixon referred to himself as a Keynesian, he did so on the basis of his balancing of the full-employment budget. Thus, at the same time that the actual budget deficit was growing rapidly, Nixon annually presented to Congress a "balanced budget at full employment."

More recently, in the 1978 *Economic Report of the President*, there was a move to drop the term "full-employment balance" and to substitute a "high-employment balance." Thus, instead of defining full employment in terms of the unemployment rate of 4 percent (which was traditional all through the sixties and early seventies), we now refer to a "high-employment unemployment rate of 4.9 percent" as the goal of economic policy makers. The underlying rationale for this acceptance of a higher unemployment rate as the goal is the change in the structure of the labor force in recent years. It is argued that there are more teenagers and women in today's labor force, and that both of these categories of workers naturally have higher unemployment rates.

This is actually truer for teenagers than it is for women. In fact, the unemployment rate for women is usually about the same as it is for men, including teenagers. In recessions it is frequently the case that the unemployment rate for women is actually less affected than the unemployment rate for men, since women are frequently employed in services, which tend to grow in recessions, while men are more often engaged in heavy industry, which is most adversely affected by a recession.

The conflict between different schools of thought now shows up in the definition of full employment. The Humphrey-Hawkins bill would define full employment in terms of a 4 percent unemployment rate, while the Carter advisers have accepted the 4.9 percent goal recommended by the outgoing Ford Administration. More conservative economists would regard something like 6 percent unemployment as the high- or full-employment rate, and therefore consider the present federal deficit as stimulative. Those economists who would prefer a full-employment unemployment rate of 4 percent could no doubt show a surplus or fiscal drag coming out of this calculation of the full-employment balance, particularly if the budgets at all three levels of government are included.

Keynesian deficit financing is less developed in postwar Japan, West Germany, and Italy. It wasn't until the 1966/67 recession that the possibilities for using deficit financing developed in the Federal Republic of Germany. In Italy, significant deficit financing was postponed until 1969 since the postwar economic policy makers were largely drawn from pre-Keynesian antifascists. And in Japan there are still legal problems preventing a bold Keynesian fiscal policy.

The emphasis on monetary fine tuning in all three countries was a postwar reaction to the Keynesian nonmonetarist solutions developed in the prewar fascist regimes. In both West Germany and Japan there has been a decline in the female labor participation rate associated with their sluggish growth in the mid-seventies.[3] This, plus the tendency to send their guest workers home, has permitted the Japanese and West German governments to maintain comparatively low official unemployment rates, despite the considerable weakness in the labor market.

Jimmy Carter was elected on a platform promising a balanced budget for 1981—clearly a retrogression from the position of the New Economists, dating back to 1962. There is great emphasis placed on reducing wasteful government spending programs. The problem with this approach is that it fails to distinguish between active and passive deficits. President Carter is still assuming that his deficits are active and caused by too much government spending. In fact, there has been a tendency for actual government expenditures to fall short of planned government expenditues in six out of the last eight years, and the under-spending in 1977 amounted to 13.7 billion dollars.[4] The cure for these passive budget deficits would appear to be more active government spending rather than less.

Q. *How did the federal debt rise so rapidly during World War II? Why was this inflationary?*

A. If we have to sell our bonds to the Federal Reserve as a buyer of last resort, this is called "monetizing the debt." These additional government bonds are the basis for a potential increase in the money supply via increased lending. The huge increases in the money supply during World War II served as a basis for the low nominal interest rates (2 percent) and the negative real interest rates after World War II until after the Treasury Accord of 1951.

Q. *Why do you say that* The Economic Consequences of the Peace *is a wrong-headed book?*

A. In short, it was not the inability of Germany to pay the reparations but the inability of the United States to receive them that constituted the problem. It is very important to recognize that there are two Keyneses: the Keynes before 1936 and the one thereafter. The first Keynes was very respectable, and that is why, when he wrote *The General Theory*, people listened to him. There were people in the economic underground who had been saying the same thing as Keynes for many years. The fact that Keynes—a respectable member of the establishment—said it, gave it weight. For example, Milton Friedman today is very complimentary about Keynes' 1930 work, the *Treatise on Money*. In other words, Keynes had a tremendous amount of skill as a pre-Keynesian economist, and *The Economic Consequences of the Peace* is a pre-Keynesian book. It is exactly the opposite of the final position of Keynes.

Q. *Is there any possibility that the United States will make good on its reparations promises to Vietnam?*

A. You might say that it would be in the interest of the United States to make good on this promise.

Q. *If Roosevelt was practicing Keynesian economics, why was there still double-digit unemployment before World War II?*

A. It is now generally believed that the New Deal was far too timid in its approach to deficit financing.

Q. *Are you saying that deficits, including the balance-of-payments deficit, are not problems for the United States?*

A. The data in the table [p. 25] provide evidence that the federal budget deficit is not a problem. That's the only reason I included these data. The recent deficit in the balance of trade and the balance-of-payments difficulties of the sixties and seventies constitute a separate problem. As Milton Friedman and others have indicated, the floating of the dollar should have eliminated the balance-of-payments problem. As recently as 1975, we had an export surplus of $10 billion, and remember that this was after the OPEC oil embargo. Thus, it's not possible to blame OPEC for the recent trade imbalance or import surplus. The import surplus may reflect stockpiling of oil (to increase our bargaining power in the long run) or simply the fact that the United States has had the best growth record since the Great Recession. The weakening of the dollar relative to the DeutscheMark, Japanese yen, and Swiss franc only stimulates our exports relative to these three countries. The greater weakness of other currencies increases their ability to export to us. I can tell you a little about the role of the multinational corporation in the trade balance. Obviously, when the multinational corporation sets up operations abroad, it uses American machines, and so all the output of machinery produced in the United States and used abroad is included in our GNP. On balance, the multinational corporation creates jobs in the United States and contributes to the export surplus. Lecture VI deals with that particular subject.

Q. *Could you clarify the difference between active and passive deficits?*

A. That's important. I'll give you an example of each. A passive deficit is brought about by unemployed labor and capital. It comes from the revenue rather than the spending side. If you are unemployed labor or capital, you can't pay taxes. So that kind of deficit is simply a reflection of the recession or weakness in the economy. It's passive in the sense that nobody made the decision to have this deficit; it's just the result of unemployed resources. I always cite the 1958 Eisenhower recession because that was a classic example. We can see from this experience that a passive deficit has no effect on inflation. That's very important. The active deficit comes about as the result of conscious decisions to increase spending by the government. As a general rule, the passive deficits are larger than the active deficits, and have been especially large in the 1970s. Active deficits are associated with *and cause* demand-pull inflation. Passive deficits are associated with *but do not cause* cost-push inflation. You won't find very many references to this, but you can find it in Walter Heller's writings in the *Wall Street Journal*. Heller is always talking about active and passive deficits. With the latter, your tax revenue falls off, and welfare and unemployment compensation go up. For every one percentage point of change in the unemployment rate you get $16 billion either up or down in taxes and $2 billion either up or down in welfare spending. And so every percentage point is worth $18 in the budget deficit. At the present time we have about 6 percent unemployment. If we brought it down to 4 percent, our total federal revenues relative to spending would go up by 2 times 18 or about $36 billion.

NOTES

[1] See *International Herald Tribune*, October 6, 1978, p. 2.

[2] The calculation of the high-employment surplus for the state and local governments was omitted from the 1978 *Economic Report of the President*, but was obtained as a result of personal correspondence with William D. Nordhaus, Member of the Council of Economic Advisers, dated August 11, 1978.

[3] One of the telling arguments for the extension of a paid "baby leave" for West German mothers was the belief that this would open up more jobs for German men.

[4] See *Economic Report of the President*, 1978, p. 64.

IV.

Unemployment and the Role of Labor

When we look at the official unemployment rate for labor, we are only looking at the tip of the underutilization iceberg. For many years we have suspected that the official unemployment rate understated the true unemployment rate. Leon Keyserling, the Chairman of the Council of Economic Advisers under President Truman, claimed that the true unemployment rate was just about double that officially recorded. During the Johnson years an effort was made to determine the true underutilization of labor by studying the subemployment rates in the ghettos, but attempts to make such calculations have been abandoned.

Still, even granting the statistical understatement of the unemployment of labor, there is probably little more undercounting today than ten years ago. Why is it, then, that we have revised our definition of full employment at a level of 4.9 percent unemployment, rather than the 4.0 percent unemployment rate assumed all through the sixties and the first half of the seventies? As mentioned already, the official explanation is that we have a higher percentage of women and teenagers in the labor force than ever before and that these two groups "naturally" have higher unemployment rates. Thus, if the labor force had the same structure as twenty years ago, our present unemployment rate might be approximately one percentage point lower than it is.

The most recent calculation shows that for the fourth quarter of 1977 the official unemployment rate was 6.6 percent, but that it would have been only 5.8 percent if we had the same labor force structure (with respect to seven demographic groups) that we had in 1956, when the actual unemployment rate was 4.0 percent.[1] In other words, 4.0 percent unemployment in 1956 is roughly equivalent to 4.9 percent unemployment in 1978. It should be mentioned that this statistical problem will be reduced in the 1980s, when as a result of the "baby bust" that began in the 1960s, teenagers will comprise a smaller percentage of the labor force.

Another problem worrying those who calculate U.S. unemployment rates is the growing discrepancy between the estimates obtained by the two principal sampling methods: (1) the 47,000 households; or (2) the 165,000 enterprises. The latter method is producing many more unemployed workers than the former. By August 1975, the difference was 625,000 unemployed persons, and it has probably grown since then. In November-December 1977, the household method showed an increase in total employment of 1.3 million persons, while the payroll data for the 165,000 concerns showed a gain of only 537,000 workers.

This tendency for the household method to understate the unemployment problem or overstate the increases in jobs as compared with the enterprise method may result from the fact that there are very large numbers of young people entering the labor force who are unable to find productive jobs in enterprises. As a result, they create their own jobs (what Galbraith refers to as self-exploitation) in the service sector. This crowding of young people into the service sector reduces the gains in labor productivity for the economy as a whole, as we shall see in Lecture IX.

Thus, the very high labor-participation rates shown for the U.S. economy in 1978 are in part a reflection of the baby boom that followed World War II and the unusually high proportion of the labor force found in the prime-age groups. What is required is an age- and sex-adjusted labor-participation rate similar to the age- and sex-adjusted unemployment rate discussed above.

The U.S. and Canadian labor unemployment rates both exhibit great regional variation. In recent years the states with good sources of energy and those selling grain to the socialist world— Texas, Wyoming, and the corn belt states—have maintained low unemployment rates, while the northeastern region of the country has tended to have high unemployment rates. In the Canadian provinces of Alberta, Saskatchewan, and Ontario there have been low unemployment rates, while the Maritime provinces and French Quebec have relatively high unemployment rates.

During the period up to 1973 it was generally assumed that the unemployment problem in the advanced capitalist world was confined to the United States and Canada. Since the Great Recession of 1974-75, however, the unemployment rates for countries outside the United States and Canada have been steadily increasing while the rate of unemployment for the United States has come down a bit under President Carter's programs, which have expanded the employment-creating CETA (Comprehensive Employment Training Act) program, defense spending, and foreign aid. The Western European unemployment rate now averages about 5.5 percent, and it is still rising. We appear to have a synchronization of unemployment rates throughout the increasingly integrated advanced capitalist system.

Above-average and double-digit unemployment rates have been suffered in Denmark, Belgium, and in parts of Great Britain, while West Germany and Switzerland have been on the low side. Nevertheless, even in West Germany there are regions with unemployment rates as high as 9 percent in early 1979. In Asia, advanced capitalist Japan is also on the low side with respect to official unemployment statistics. The latter three countries' success, however, has been achieved at the expense of their guest workers, including women.[2] Japan, in particular, has applied great pressure on women to resume their traditional household roles. Thus, when indicators of social well-being (including household work as a plus) are compared for the 1960s and 1970s, it can be shown that there has been an increase in welfare (for Japanese males) despite the slowdown in the overall growth of the economy.[3]

As bad as unemployment rates have been outside the United States in the past five years, they would have looked even worse were it not for the fact that there has been a sharp decline in productivity increases. A recent calculation in the London *Econ-*

omist shows that for the seven most advanced capitalist countries disguised unemployment has increased faster than overt unemployment.[4] If we had experienced a continuation of 1960-73 productivity increases for the past five years, we would have had 41.8 million unemployed rather than the 13.2 million actually recorded. For every unemployed worker in these seven countries, there are roughly two others who constitute disguised unemployment, as can be seen in the table.

It is frequently argued that the unemployment problem in the advanced capitalist system can be traced to the higher energy costs which began in 1974, but this analysis overlooks the fact that even the countries that are self-sufficient with respect to petroleum (Canada and Norway, for example) have not escaped the crisis. Failure to lower taxes to offset the deflationary impact of the oil price increase no doubt exacerbated the overall problem, but there would appear to be something more fundamentally awry with the system.

Overt and Disguised Unemployment in the Advanced Capitalist System, 1978

Country	Overt unemployment (million persons)	Predicted unemployment[a] (million persons)	Disguised unemployment (million persons)	Index of minimization of disguised unemployment[b]
(1)	(2)	(3)	(4)	(5)
United States	6.1	14.0	7.9	44
Federal Republic of Germany	1.0	2.7	1.7	37
Japan	1.2	12.6	11.4	10
Great Britain	1.4	3.6	2.2	39
France	1.1	2.5	1.4	44
Italy	1.5	5.0	3.5	30
Canada	0.9	1.4	0.5	64
Total	13.2	41.8	28.6	32

Source: "Unemployment in Disguise," *The Economist*, October 21, 1978, pp. 105-06.

[a]Assuming 1960-73 productivity growth for 1973-78.

[b]Column 2 as a percent of Column 3. A lower index indicates greater disguised unemployment and a weaker labor market, and a sharper decline in the rate of increase in labor productivity. A higher index indicates a lesser amount of disguised unemployment and a stronger labor market, as well as a lesser decline in the rate of increase in labor productivity.

As in the United States, teenagers and young college graduates in Western Europe are more than proportionately affected by the impact of the unemployment problem. The entry of a higher percentage of young people into the universities merely postpones the problem and fosters alienation in various forms, including terrorism.

It is interesting to compare explanations for capitalist unemployment at various stages of our economic development. In the early thirties it was popular to assume that wages were too high in relationship to a so-called equilibrium wage. If only wages could be reduced, urged the celebrated British economist Pigou, more jobs could be created. The economists in the Weimar Republic's Brüning government, including the revisionist Marxist Rudolf Hilferding, actually put into effect such a policy, convincing German workers that they should all take a 10 percent cut in wages. Herbert Hoover, to his everlasting credit, saw wages as an important source of purchasing power and refused to emulate the Germans.

By 1933 the Germans were experiencing unemployment rates of over 40 percent, while the official unemployment rate for the United States was in the neighborhood of 25 percent. Actually, we had very poor unemployment statistics at the time, since unemployment compensation—now used as an important basis for estimating unemployment—didn't exist in the United States until 1935. The United States didn't develop unemployment compensation until five years after the Soviet Union had abandoned this basically capitalist institution.

This pre-Keynesian approach to the unemployment problem is still found in the writings of the New Right. According to their position, minimum-wage laws and too-generous unemployment compensation are the root cause of unemployment: it's not the shortage of jobs, but the lack of incentive to take unpleasant jobs and jobs beneath one's qualifications, that is to blame. Conservatives in the Council of Economic Advisers also blame recent laws reducing discrimination against minorities for an increase in unemployment. Their argument sounds something like this. If only blacks and other minorities could be hired at lower wages, as they formerly were, their unemployment rates would stop rising relative to white male unemployment rates.

At the beginning of the sixties, after eight years of Eisenhower drifting, unemployment began to receive top attention, particularly since other capitalist countries, excluding Canada, had much lower unemployment rates. At one point President Kennedy sent his top economic advisers to Western Europe to find out the secret of their success. The argument at this time was over whether the unemployment was due to lack of aggregate demand or to so-called structural problems in the labor market. Some economists, such as Charles Killingsworth, argued that rapid technological changes were producing requirements for a labor force possessing new and different skills. The rapid increases in labor productivity at the time lent some substance to this claim.

However, the New Economists chiefly opted for the approach of increasing aggregate demand. By the time the manpower training programs of the War on Poverty actually went into effect in the latter half of the sixties, the economy was already near full employment. Thus, such training programs—involving up to one million persons in training, administering and moving from one retraining program to another—simply disguised the fact that we didn't really have full employment during most of the Vietnam War. The Johnson Administration also began to disregard the unemployment of any person below 16 years of age or anyone who had not taken overt steps to find a job within the preceding four weeks.

One of the obvious differences between the diagnoses of the seventies and those of the early sixties is that no one is presently blaming rapid technological change and technological unemployment for our difficulties. The sluggish productivity increases since 1966 have apparently eliminated the possibility of blaming rapid technological change. Instead, conventional wisdom, like that in W. W. Rostow's recent book, argues that we must *step up* the rate of investment, research, and development, and the rate of technological change, to get us "from here to there."

In the union movement the solutions usually advocated are protectionist and nationalist, rather than internationalist. It is argued that Americans should "buy American" (International Ladies' Garment Workers); that multinational corporations should be restrained from investing abroad; that protectionist tariffs or import controls should be stepped up; or that we should tighten our immigration laws and/or round up illegal immigrants and send them home. Naturally, there is no great enthusiasm for progressive replacement of men by machines under present labor-market conditions, as there was in the immediate postwar years under the leadership of progressives such as Walter Reuther.

Workers are also unenthusiastic about environmental protection laws and protests against the spread of nuclear power, since they value their own jobs above the ultimate welfare of their neighbors or even their own families. Neither is there much enthusiasm about East-West trade, despite the fact that on balance more jobs could be created by its expansion. Apparently the wave of economic isolationism arising from intracapitalist world trade has spilled over into this area.[5]

Even more important than the unemployment of labor, however, is the unemployment of capital, as reflected in the capacity-utilization rate. The true amount of capital unemployment in the U.S. economy has been disguised by several statistical revisions conducted by the Federal Reserve Board. But in both Japan and Western Europe the unrevised capacity-utilization rates are considerably lower than those for the United States. As a result of the failure to spread overhead costs properly, unit overhead costs rise as an important ingredient of cost-push inflation.

Q. *Why is it necessary to adjust crude data?*

A. We might call these calculations the age- and sex-adjusted unemployment or full-employment unemployment rate. I'll give you an example. One of the current examples is the fact that the crime rate in the United States is falling. What you have to do is to age-adjust the crime rate. In other words, crime tends to be committed by young people, and we have had a great many young people in our mature population. And now that we will have the effect of the baby bust, we can predict that the United States crime rate will continue to fall if you do not adjust for age. You are probably familiar with the same phenomenon in connection with crude death rates. For example, Puerto Rico has a lower crude death rate than the United States. Do you understand the reason why Puerto Rico has a lower crude death rate than the United States and probably the lowest in the world? They have very few old people, and the low crude death rate reflects the impact of modern medicine and lots of young people. The Soviet Union's crude death rate fell for a long time, but it is now rising because the population is getting older. So you always have to be sure to age-adjust population death rates, crime rates, etc. It really doesn't mean anything to talk about crude death rates. The German Democratic Republic which has very good medical service but an old population, has a very high crude death rate.

Q. *Why does the northeastern section of the United States have high unemployment rates? For example, Rhode Island had a 16 percent unemployment rate not too long ago.*

A. Capital after World War II tended to leave the region and relocate in the South or Sunbelt where labor was relatively unorganized. The closing of military bases has also been a factor in this area.

Q. *Why is there so much criticism of CETA?*

A. CETA is subject to much criticism because many people think that their employment is like leaf-raking during the Great Depression.

Q. *Why are Western policy makers interested in greater synchronization?*

A. Integration or synchronization can have a good or a bad meaning. If you are talking about unemployment, it happens to be bad for Western Europe. If you're talking about inflation, it might be a good thing for the United States. In other words, it's impossible for a member of the advanced capitalist system to isolate itself from the group. Presumably, all the advanced capitalist countries can be pursuing the same policy at the same time if there is greater synchronization.

Q. *What are socioeconomic indicators, and how do they measure welfare?*

A.   They include such things as the condition of the air, health, education, etc. If you don't have enough industrial jobs for people, obviously the factory smoke and environmental pollution will be less. People staying in school longer may be a positive socioeconomic indicator, or it may simply reflect disguised unemployment.

Q.   *What is the meaning of the data in the Table [p. 37]?*

A.   This table is very important in substantiating my hypothesis that Japan and West Germany are the weakest links of the advanced capitalist system—weakest in the sense that they have the most disguised unemployment. In other words, they have pushed their women back into the home. You also have to remember that the West Germans sent home their guest workers from Southern Europe.

Q.   *What about the Soviet Union? Is our high labor-participation rate for women positive?*

A.   Your very high labor participation rate would indicate that you have very little disguised unemployment. I don't see any Soviet women returning to their homes. I think that only one country has a higher percentage of women in the labor force, and that is the German Democratic Republic.

Q.   *What is the purpose of the calculation in Column 5 of the Table?*

A.   These figures show the relative ability of the countries to maintain the rate of productivity increase for the period indicated. The higher figure in Column 5 would indicate that the decline in productivity growth is less than it is for Japan. Japanese productivity was growing by about 14 percent a year from 1960 to 1973. Since then it has dropped down to 4 percent, a great decline. The purpose of this calculation is to show that the situation outside the United States and Canada is much worse than it is in these two countries. We haven't sent our guest workers home. On the contrary, we're accepting more and more illegal immigrants. Our women are still increasing as a percentage of the total labor force. They are not going back into the home as they are in Japan and West Germany. My hypothesis is that the reason for the weakness of Japan and West Germany is what happened to their currency. The strength of their currencies in the eyes of bankers and currency speculators produces a weakness in their economies.

Q. *Why has the OPEC price increase produced problems in the advanced capitalist system?*

A. Let me emphasize again that the increase in OPEC prices is like an increase in excise taxes, and in order to offset that "shock" the system has to reduce taxes or increase spending. If you have an increase in tax coming from abroad, your domestic policy has to move in the other direction. And none of the advanced capitalist countries had either the insight or the political ability to reduce taxes. If you raise taxes, it deflates the economy and increases unemployment. So in order to avoid that you can lower tax rates if you understand Keynesian economics.

Q. *If you reduce taxes, won't demand rise?*

A. Yes, that's exactly what it should do.

Q. *But aren't both the growth of demand and the rising oil prices related to inflation?*

A. I'm afraid you haven't yet learned the difference between demand-pull and cost-push. That is fundamental. The increase in oil prices or excise taxes is a type of cost-push inflation. If you remember, in my lecture I said that you have a choice between cost-push and demand-pull. And it's much better to have demand-pull than cost-push. So that's precisely what we want to do: to lower other taxes, increase demand, and get back to demand-pull inflation.

Q. *Do you believe in so-called structural unemployment?*

A. I didn't believe in it in the first place when the issue was raised in the early sixties. I thought it was nonsense then, and I think that what has happened since then has confirmed this. I think most any job— except the economist's—can be learned in a week.

Q. *If you control wages for some period of time, can't you control unemployment?*

A. That's the same kind of thinking that got us into the Great Depression. We also got Hitler because of that way of thinking. Germany followed such a policy by holding down wages to create employment. It's a classic example of pre-Keynesian thinking.

Q. *Doesn't West Germany use this technique of holding back wages with the result that their real rate of unemployment appears to be less than others?*

A. Most experiences with incomes policies in the West have been failures. They last for about one or two years. The only country that has a successful incomes policy is the Soviet Union. But you haven't always had a successful incomes policy. It's only since World War II that you've had a successful incomes policy. In the 1930s, wages increased by 20 percent a year in the Soviet Union. Productivity increased by 5 or 6 percent yearly. And so you had terrible inflation, but you didn't know you had inflation because you stopped publishing the cost-of-living index in 1930.

NOTES

[1] See *Economic Report of the President, 1978*, p. 170. We might call this the age and sex-adjusted unemployment or full employment unemployment rate. The same adjustment has been made in crude death rates for many years. It should also be applied to such things as crime rates, which on the surface are falling.

[2] See "Exploring the Underground Economy," *The Economist*, September 22-28, 1979, p. 106. In 1977, the indexes of economically active women (ages 15-64) with 1965 = 100 were as follows: Japan—95; Federal Republic of Germany—99; France—112; Great Britain—117; Italy—119; United States—126; and Canada—144.

[3] The true Japanese unemployment rate is apparently much higher than the 2 percent usually cited. According to the *Wall Street Journal*, April 9, 1979: "Some labor experts estimate that as many as 6 million—12 percent of the labor force—are unemployed or the equivalent of unemployed, which means that workers are paid salaries without having a productive job in the economy."

[4] "Unemployment in Disguise," *The Economist*, October 21, 1978, pp. 105-06.

[5] The influence of the ex-Communist Jay Lovestone as adviser to George Meany has no doubt been involved in slowing down the increase in East-West trade.

V.

Market and Plan in Agriculture and Industry

Socialists have frequently debated the respective roles to be played by the plan and the market in their system. This issue is to date less obvious in the advanced capitalist system, but it nevertheless exists. Perhaps the decade when market forces were operating to their fullest extent in the advanced capitalist system was the twenties. The business of America was business, and the role of government was inconsequential.

The twenties were a decade of great prosperity, not only in the United States but also in France, and especially in Germany (following her brief experience with hyperinflation in 1923). Only Canada had a better growth record than Germany. Great Britain was an exception in this regard since her double-digit unemployment was chronic, in part due to the overvaluation of the pound at its prewar value.

Although the U.S. economy grew rapidly in the twenties, there were minor recessions in 1921, 1924, and 1927. Labor productivity increases were especially rapid in this decade, averaging about 6 percent per year—the most rapid advancement in our economic history. At the same time, money wages were increasing by only 3 percent yearly, so that unit labor costs and prices were falling. Profits were buoyant and were promptly reinvested in new capacity, so that by the end of the decade there was considerable excess capacity. Consumption was weakened by the relatively slow increase in money wages.[1]

Another area of great weakness in the United States in the twenties was agriculture. Agriculture had overexpanded under the seller's market conditions of World War I, so that the twenties were generally characterized as a decade of surplus agricultural product with depressed prices and incomes. While the rest of the economy prospered, the same could not be said for our farmers.

The weakness of agricultural prices was also important in accounting for the lack of inflation in consumers' prices, which actually declined by 3 percent during the decade. This combination of very rapid economic growth and falling prices was unique in twentieth-century capitalist economic history. Nostalgia for this period shows up in the writings of Walt W. Rostow, who confesses a weakness for declining prices. In Rostow's words: "I believe that, for our times, the optimum solution would be a regime of fixed money wages, with prices falling with the increase in productivity."[2]

The Great Depression greatly exacerbated American farmers' problems, since agricultural prices fell sharply in the deflation of 1929-33, while industrial prices of the things farmers buy were sticky. Large industrialists showed an ability to reduce their output and retain their prices as the Depression deepened. By the time of the New Deal, it became obvious that the market system was malfunctioning, and government planning was required for both agriculture and industry.

In agriculture the result was the Agricultural Adjustment Act (AAA), which provided for various sorts of programs to reduce the agricultural surplus, including the "killing of little pigs" by the Secretary of Agriculture, Henry Wallace. Surplus agricultural produce was burned or destroyed at a time when the urban population was either selling apples on street corners or standing in line for soup.

Planning for industry took the form of the National Recovery Act (NRA), which was modeled after Mussolini's corporate state apparatus.[3] Competition and market forces were to be reduced, and the role of the state was to be greatly strengthened. Labor unions, of declining importance in the twenties, were encouraged by the New Deal, and a shorter work week was decreed to spread the existing jobs around among more people. Legislation such as the Robinson-Patman Act and the Miller-

Tydings Enabling Act was designed to regulate "unfair competition," a euphemism for reducing competition and market forces. Restrictions on competitive market forces coming from abroad were also widespread, and a "Buy American" protectionist ideology was the rule.

The United States entered World War II with huge inventories of various agricultural products that had been taken off the market to support agricultural prices at levels higher than the competitive market would allow. In the nonagricultural sector there were ample supplies of unemployed and underemployed labor, as well as considerable excess productive capacity. The experience of World War II ultimately showed that prewar estimates of underutilization actually understated the overall realization problem. The steel industry during the war operated at 120 percent of this supposed capacity.

The wartime economic boom in the United States gradually liquidated the agricultural surpluses. The government began to sell off agricultural stocks when market prices rose above a level that was supposedly designed to give the farmer "parity" with industrial prices, as defined by the relative price relationship during the years 1910-14. By the end of World War II the surplus stocks had been eliminated, and agricultural prices were considered solidly above parity. The immediate postwar shipments of wheat and other foods under the United Nations Relief and Rehabilitation (UNRRA) program also contributed to firmer prices for U.S. agriculture. Incidentally, some of this UNRRA wheat found its way to Eastern Europe.

Whereas most studies of industrial concentration made in the thirties (the most celebrated of which was that of Adolf Berle and Gardiner Means) suggested that monopoly power was increasing, the postwar studies showed that the planned full-employment economy of World War II had somehow resuscitated competition in the market place. By 1950 Warren Nutter, for example, was able to show that there had really been no increase in industrial concentration since 1900.

The postwar years in agriculture witnessed a sharp increase in productivity, in part due to the cheapening of fertilizer as a result of technological changes during the war, and in part because of the substitution of machine for muscle. The development of corporate agricultural organization and the application of industrial management techniques has also been a factor increasing agricultural efficiency. As a result, during the past thirty years, agricultural labor productivity has grown by about 5 percent per annum.

As a consequence of the upsurge in agricultural productivity, there has been a rapid exodus of surplus manpower out of agriculture, so that now only about 4 percent of the U.S. labor force remains in this sector. In the Commonwealth of Puerto Rico, the agricultural exodus has been so rapid that agriculture now employs only 3 percent of the island's working age population. This exodus has been partly subsidized by agricultural surpluses on the mainland, since about 60 percent of the Puerto Rican population receive food stamps.[4]

This tremendous increase in agricultural productivity naturally created surplus stocks. At first, they were stored in Liberty Ships in the Hudson River. But when the grain began to rot and was infested with rats, it became obvious that this was an imperfect solution. As a result of the war and the emergence of the United States as the most powerful world economy, our international trade position took a 180 degree turn. Instead of our traditional protectionism, the United States—like Great Britain in the nineteenth century—became the preeminent advocate of freer trade. The agency most responsible for carrying out this trade policy was the General Agreement on Tariffs and Trade (GATT). The world market for agricultural produce would presumably absorb the growing domestic surplus.

If the world commercial sales of agricultural produce were still inadequate, then the surplus could be given away under Public Law 480, as has been explained in Lecture III. As in the thirties, restrictions on the planting—soil banks and acreage set asides—or marketing of certain crops came back to reduce the magnitude of the surplus-disposal problem. In more recent times, there have also been domestic possibilities for giving free or cheaper foods away to poverty-stricken families. The present plan calls for food stamps to be given to all individuals and families whose incomes fall below a certain level. In past times, there were some families too poor even to afford food stamps (which required some cash outlays), but the Carter Administration has recently removed this inequity.

The devaluation of the dollar in 1971 produced a sudden expansion of demand for U.S. agricultural products on world markets. At the same time, the stocks of agricultural surpluses were comparatively low, more or less in accordance with the planned acreage restrictions on United States farmers. A final stimulus to U.S. agricultural sales abroad came about as a result of the poor agricultural harvest in the Soviet Union in 1972.

As a result of these stimuli, agricultural prices skyrocketed, both within and outside the United States. During 1973-75, agricultural prices and incomes in the United States were substantially higher, and there was unparalleled prosperity in the midwestern states. In 1973, per capita disposable personal income of the farm population actually exceeded that of the nonfarm population for a brief time.[5] In effect, the United States nearly achieved a goal of communism: it had almost evened out the difference between rural and urban standards of living.

President Nixon, to his credit, saw in this temporary shortage of agricultural produce an opportunity to remove crop restrictions on U.S. farmers. Henceforth, our agricultural sector was generally to be encouraged to grow as much as it possibly could, in order to restore the world's agricultural stocks. Should a new surplus develop in the future—which in fact it did— Nixon introduced something equivalent to the Benson-Brannon Plan, which had been proposed by President Truman's Secretary of Agriculture in the late 1940s. Instead of holding up farm prices and damaging export possibilities, Nixon's plan provided that prices would be allowed to fall, and   vernment check would be written in favor of the farmer to the extent that the prices realized failed to reach some "fair" level.

In order to regulate grain sales to the USSR, an agreement was signed according to which the Soviets pledged to import at least a minimum amount yearly over a long-term period. Instead of giving so much grain away under Public Law 480, U.S. policy was now to make more commercial sales abroad via the devalued dollar and the planned sales to the USSR. If the dollar continued to depreciate, as it did to some extent, so much the better for the prices at which the United States could export, at least to Japan, West Germany, and Switzerland.

Japan, in particular, has been under great pressure to accept U.S. meat and oranges. The Japanese government has enacted a new set of subsidies that will pay farmers to tear out their mandarin orange groves. Thus, American oranges—which are in tremendous oversupply—can now be exported to Japan.[6]

President Carter's agricultural program has once again brought a return of some acreage restrictions, as grain production burgeoned and prices fell in 1977. Roughly 20 percent of grain land is to be removed from cultivation. In April 1977, the Administration also announced the formation of a small food-grain reserve of 8 million metric tons of wheat and rice, which was enlarged to 30-35 million tons in August of the same year. This reserve system is to be owned and held to a large extent by farmers themselves, with the government sharing the cost of holding the reserve. Driving through the Midwest, one sees on many farms a small forest of blue grain-storage silos with the American flag painted on top.

Advanced capitalist countries in Western Europe and Japan likewise tend to subsidize and protect their agricultural producers. In addition, they are also subject to the growth of surpluses, as exemplified by the West German "butter mountain" that was reduced by sales to Eastern Europe. In Japan there is a tremendous rice surplus problem. The Japanese government buys rice from farmers at $1,500 per ton and sells it to consumers at a 15 percent discount. Any additional unsold rice is sold back to farmers to feed their livestock at $150 per ton or dumped abroad at $350 per ton.

The less-developed capitalist countries may also produce agricultural surpluses that depress agricultural prices relative to industrial prices—the so-called international price scissors. This is increasingly evident in other countries such as India, which has begun to harvest "miracle rice" developed by the Ford Foundation in Mexico. Thus far, international commodity agreements have tended to cartelize the sale of agricultural products such as coffee and sugar, with each participating country agreeing to export not more than a certain quota in order to keep prices from falling on world markets. The underdeveloped countries are demanding a New International Economic Order coming out of the United Nations Conference on Trade and Development (UNCTAD), which would involve the creation of a common fund to finance operations designed to plan world buffer stocks and the sales of 17 commodities, both agricultural commodities and raw materials.

Until recently, the United States and other advanced capitalist countries have preferred commodity-by-commodity approaches to this problem, but this may be changing. The final statement of the recent Bonn summit meeting contains a positive evaluation of the proposed "Common Fund."[7]

The problem of industrial concentration and monopoly power after World War II was also affected by the new U.S. position on the importance of free trade and increased reliance on foreign suppliers. Whereas concentration ratios made some sense in the thirties when the United States was rather protectionist, they became virtually meaningless in the postwar years. For example, a domestic concentration ratio is certainly meaningless for the automobile industry, with Japan and Western Europe producing for the United States market along with the Big Three domestic automobile makers. In other words, U.S. corporations were henceforth to be kept on their toes by foreign competition rather than by the breaking down of large oligopolies.

Official U.S. policy with respect to concentration and monopoly power is that one of the purposes of government is to restrict or restrain monopoly. Beginning with the Sherman Act of 1890 and the Clayton Act some 24 years later, it has been assumed that the Federal Trade Commission and the Anti-Trust Division of the Department of Justice were designed to do just this. Judging by the record, however, one cannot help but be a bit skeptical of the U.S. antitrust program. While the two organizations do provide considerable employment for both economists and lawyers, they always seem to be attacking some inconspicuous local monopoly such as the lobster fishermen in Maine.

According to one school of thought, led by Gabriel Kolko, the whole idea of regulating monopolies was conjured up by the monopolies themselves, in an effort to restrict the ruinous "unfair" competition of the market. The evidence for this position is particularly strong in the case of regulating agencies such as the Interstate Commerce Commission, which is clearly designed to reduce competition and create employment through waste.

One interesting bit of antitrust legislation, the Celler-Kefauver Act of 1950, did produce some effect on industrial concentration. By restricting mergers that tended to increase either vertical or horizontal monopoly in an industry, it helped foster the growth of the conglomerate corporation engaging in operations in many industries. Thus, while there doesn't seem to be any tendency for ordinary concentration ratios in different industries to show either increasing or decreasing competition or concentration, there is a tendency for the share of the total industrial output accounted for by the top 200 corporations (many of which are conglomerates) to rise. Nevertheless, we should not forget the fact that the service sector—which is largely competitive and, to a great extent, subject to market forces—is the most rapidly growing part of the total economy. Thus, monopolies do not seem to pose a serious threat to our economic well-being.

Finally, we should also be somewhat skeptical about the role of the oligopoly in causing the recent inflation. A government study of the years up to 1970 showed that the price increases in the oligopolistic sectors were less than they were in the non-oligopolistic sectors. Apparently, the greater relative efficiency of the oligopolies has permitted them to keep down costs and prices in an era when cost-push inflation increasingly dominates price movements.

It is also interesting to note that certain other advanced capitalist countries get along without comparable antitrust activities. In fact, the tendency in recent years is for Great Britain and France to encourage, rather than discourage, the merging of their industrial giants in order for them to compete more effectively with corporations in other advanced capitalist countries, principally the United States.

The underlying problem in the case of agriculture and industry is that the demand curves for so many products, and especially agricultural commodities, are inelastic, at least in the short run. Under these conditions, a reduction in supply—whether by holocaust or planned government action, such as the burning of coffee by Brazilian governments—tends to increase total revenues and prosperity.

In the case of industrial prices, firms are reluctant to reduce prices, fearing that this may set off a so-called "price war." Instead, the substitution of nonprice competition or advertising is considered more acceptable, even though it may reduce profits rather than increase consumer prices. When the government forced the cigarette industry to stop advertising on television several years ago, there was an immediate increase in the profits of cigarette manufacturers. To the extent that the demand curves of the products are inelastic in the short run, there is always a built-in bias in favor of raising prices, and in the process, total revenues.

We have seen that in the past 70 years the United States has fluctuated between reliance on the market and on increased government intervention or planning, designed to reduce or hold back the agricultural surplus. More and more, however, the ebb-and-flow movement seems to be away from market forces and in the direction of government controls and planning. The movement toward industrial planning has been slower but is perhaps also inevitable.[8]

Q. *Why is Peter Temin's book* [Did Monetary Forces Cause the Great Depression?] *important?*

A. Peter Temin's book, which came out in 1976, documents the weakness of consumption at the beginning of the Great Depression (1930). This is an answer to the Friedman argument that monetary policy caused the Great Depression. By the way, do you know which leader of the Soviet Union believed in the policy of falling prices, as preferred by Rostow? [Silence.] Your prices actually fell from 1947 to 1954. Stalin believed in falling prices as early as the first five-year plan but was unable to carry out this policy until after World War II.

Q.   *How do you measure monopoly power in the United States?*

A.   We use concentration ratios to measure monopoly power. One measure might be: what percentage of the total sales are accounted for by the top four firms?

Q.   *What were Liberty ships?*

A.   Liberty ships were built very rapidly during the war, mainly by women—who were welcomed into the labor force. Women for the first time came into the U.S. industrial labor force during World War II. Henry Kaiser was the man responsible for this phenomenon. The ships were functional, but that's about all you can say for them. They were very poorly put together. However, this is not a reflection on women's labor.

Q.   *What is a price scissors?*

A.   You will remember that you had a domestic price scissors in the twenties. Industrial prices were on the top blade of the scissors, and agricultural prices represented the lower blade. As a result, you had a "scissors crisis" when your farmers preferred not to market their grain and instead consumed it in greater proportions.

Q.   *What is the price per ton of the wheat that you export to other countries?*

A.   That's a technical question, and I'm afraid I don't know the precise answer. I know the price per bushel, since we usually price wheat per bushel. Roughly speaking, it's about $2.50 per bushel. I know you use metric tons, but we use bushels. It's a fair price, not a high price. As you know, we don't have the metric system yet. We are theoretically changing to the metric system, but in all societies there is great resistance to change.

Q.   *Agricultural production in both the United States and Western Europe is out of proportion. What accounts for this? Is the blame to be put on the market or on the plan?*

A.   I would say it is a reflection of the inadequacies of the distribution system in both the United States and Western Europe. Our income distribution is comparatively inflexible. If we moved toward greater equality, we would be able to clear the market and free people to move to more productive areas. This is a reflection of the contradiction between production and distribution. The American system has a tremendous ability to produce goods. But the problem is how do you get income into the hands of the people with the most need. There is also an international distribution problem. One of the things that would happen if we got the New International Economic Order (NIEO) Common Fund would be that the underdeveloped countries would have more purchasing power to buy our surpluses. In other words, the world income distribution would be more equal and allow for the absorption of this tremendous productive potential. We have two possibilities in this area. In the past, we gave surplus food away under Public Law 480 and used this gift in a political way. In other words, a country that didn't vote the way it should in the United Nations would have its food cut off. If you had the NIEO and fair prices for the 17 materials, you wouldn't have to give the food away, but you would lose political power. In the last analysis, it's a struggle for political power between the advanced capitalist countries and the Third World.

Q.   *Why do you have this overproduction of agricultural produce? Is it because of mistakes in plans or is it due to weak organization?*

A.   Do you mean if we had more of a monopoly, we could control the supply? That's essentially Galbraith's point, I think. He would like to have all sectors of the economy organized pretty much in the same way that agriculture is organized by the government. You can do it by the private sector as you do in industry or you can have government stepping in and performing the same role for agriculture, or for the service sector for that matter. You could have government intervention in all sectors, improving the monopoly position of the competitive sectors, such as agriculture, etc. Galbraith wants to model the rest of the sectors on the agricultural. Our agricultural sector is tremendously successful in terms of productivity. This is a planned sector and it is very successful. Productivity is growing the fastest in the monopoly sectors. You can do it two ways. You can do it through the private sector, that is, the monopoly sector, or you can do it through government, organizing the competitive sectors, as they have agriculture. In Galbraith's last book, he talks about organizing everybody else so that you can get more efficiency there too. Everybody knows that the competitive sector, particularly the service sector, is the most inefficient part of our system. And so we would have the government perform the same role in the service sector that it already is doing in agriculture. Still, you have to remember that you have the distribution problem. That is the tough nut to cräck. We have solved our production problems. But we haven't solved our distribution problems.

Q. *What percent of agricultural products are produced by corporate farms?*

A. There's a figure in the *Economic Report of the President*, which as I recall, may be that about 15 percent of the farms produce about 57 percent of the total output. I believe that was roughly the figure. It's interesting that the corporate farm hasn't developed as rapidly as most people had thought it would. The small family farm is still heavily subsidized by the federal government. We have an ideology that puts the small family farm on a pedestal. Our sociologists are always praising the noneconomic advantages of the small family farm. The problem here is that most of the people who praise the small family farm have never been on a small family farm. I was raised on a small family farm and I can tell you, it's no paradise. One of the interesting new developments is a special law that exempts $160,000 of farm assets on the small family farm from inheritance taxes. In other words, when they thought the inheritance tax was a threat to the small family farm, protection was sought through legislation.

Q. *How do you define the small family farm?*

A. In the United States a small family farm may represent an investment of $200,000. That's the minimum in the grain belt. The average size of a farm in the United States today is probably between 300 and 400 acres.

Q. *Isn't it true that this Celler Act was passed after vertical and horizontal concentration had already taken place?*

A. That's true, but it did stop it. It could have continued. There is no necessary upper limit to horizontal and vertical merging. It certainly stopped well below 100 percent. We can't prove it, but if we hadn't had the Celler Act it's entirely possible that the concentration ratios would have increased. They haven't increased. Some have gone down, as a matter of fact.

Q. *It is not quite enough to take the percentage of total employment by the top four firms.*

A. It's true, and you can use different measures of concentration. You can use sales, capital, value-added, etc., as above. In other words, there are many different methods.

Q. *What about the third wave of mergers, which started after the Vietnam War?*

A. I think that the concentration problem increases as growth slows down. I consider concentration a secondary problem to the growth problem. If you had proper fiscal policy the concentration problem wouldn't exist, as we found in World War II. World War II increased the amount of competition tremendously by just getting the economy growing again. I think that what has happened since 1970 in terms of increased mergers and increased concentration is a function of the overall economic problem, particularly the Great Recession of 1974-75. In economics we always have the problem of distinguishing between cause and effect. And I feel that concentration is an effect, not a cause, a secondary symptom of something more fundamental.

Q. *The National Bureau of Economic Research published the findings of a conference which was held in 1973 at Princeton University. They said that it's not possible to plan the mergers or to plan antitrust policy.*

A. I never heard of this. I'm not familiar with this particular conference. Every conference sets out to prove something, and they usually invite people who will say what they want them to say. I'd be curious to see who was there. France and England are actually encouraging mergers. I think that antitrust is a peculiarly American hang-up. Antitrust is an American fetish. We have this dilemma of liking small firms, but we also like efficiency. So we have this problem, because it is the large firm that is efficient.

Q. *What possibility do you see for introducing government planning in industry?*

A. In order for planning to work in any advanced capitalist country there has to be an interference with investment. That's the key area that has to be planned. Unless that is done, we won't really have planning. Take somebody like Rostow, who wants to introduce planning only in the energy sector. He thinks that if you have this huge energy sector planned that everything else will somehow fall into place. That's possible, but I'm very skeptical of that position. It's the areas that fluctuate in investment that are important.

Q. *What do you think about the policy of the present administration toward energy? Will it increase concentration in this sector?*

A. I think it probably will. If you're going to have planning, it's easier to plan with a few large units than with many small ones. The energy sector is already concentrated. The oil companies are in the coal business, as well as nuclear power and all sorts of other energy sources. They already have taken over the various alternatives. It's already very concentrated. I don't think it needs to be much more concentrated.

Q. *Do you think that if the concentration ratio in energy increases, it will affect the concentration ratios of other sectors?*

A. I'm not a specialist in this area.

Q. *To what degree is the large firm efficient? What are the limits to this efficiency?*

A. I think if you look at the automobile industry, it's quite clear that General Motors, which accounts for about half of all the domestic production—more than half, actually—is by far the most efficient, and there is no evidence that this advantage is being reduced. I think that there are tremendous economies of scale that are being brought about by the computerization of management. It used to be that the management decision-making problem limited the size of firms, and I think that the computer has enlarged the possibility of successful management on a very, very large scale.

Q. *Is this true with regard to an absolute monopoly in an industry?*

A. Well, theoretically, General Motors has to really fight to avoid being a monopoly. There have to be special laws created to keep American Motors alive. American Motors [and now Chrysler—L.T.] would not exist if it were not for special legislation as well as special trade union considerations. They pay lower wages than General Motors. General Motors is a highly successful firm that has to struggle not to become a monopoly—because that would be opposed to the American way of doing things.

Q. *What about Ford?*

A. Ford is clearly in another league. A friend of mine has worked as an economist for both GM and Ford and he claims there was a world of difference. At GM, he had a relaxed 40-hour week; at Ford, they had to struggle to recapture their share of the market.

Q. *Is it possible for General Motors to become a monopoly?*

A. I don't think so, as long as Congress interferes. Without the interference of Congress, that would be the logical thing to happen, were it not for our ideology, which says that monopoly is a bad thing, and we have to have at least competition among the few. That's what oligopoly is. As William Fellner has written, oligopoly can be defined as competition among the few.

Q. *What are the real results of antitrust laws? They seem to have done very little.*

A. I think they chiefly create jobs for lawyers and economists.

Q. *What was Marx's position on monopoly?*

A. Marx thought that the increased monopolization was a good thing, because he thought it would be easier to socialize a large corporation than a lot of small corporations.

NOTES

[1] See Peter Temin, *Did Monetary Forces Cause the Great Depression?*, W. W. Norton, 1976. It should be noted that Temin specifically rejects the "underconsumptionist" implications of his research. It is traditional for both conventional and Marxist theoreticians to reject underconsumptionist conclusions.

[2] W. W. Rostow, *Getting From Here to There*, McGraw-Hill, New York, 1978, p. 205. This was also the favorite price policy of Joseph Stalin, who managed to follow such a policy from 1947 until his death in 1953.

[3] In this connection, see Martha Weissman Lear, "On Harry, and Henry and Ike and Dr. Shaw," *New York Times Magazine*, April 22, 1973, p. 49. In this interview, Claire Booth Luce says: "Friends had brought me the English translation of a book by Amintore Fanfani, who was the economic think-man for Mussolini. It was the distillation of the philosophy by which Mussolini rescued Italy from the shambles of approaching Communist chaos. Well, America was in chaos at that point. It was six months after the election of Roosevelt, with that terrible Depression going on. I underlined various sections of this book and took it to General (Hugh) Johnson. We met in Dinty Moore's, I remember,

and right in that restaurant, on those red-and-white checkered tablecloths he sketched out N.R.A.—the National Recovery Administration—and right out of Fanfani's book. He brought it to Roosevelt, and Roosevelt bought it lock, stock,and barrel. You see, the origins of the first New Deal were never leftist. They were a socialism of the right, to begin with."

[4] As a result of lower maximum incomes, 53.3 percent of the population received food stamps worth $880 million or 10 percent of the U.S. food stamp funds. See *New York Times*, "Food Stamps Buoying Economy in Puerto Rico," May 12, 1979, p. 9.

[5] *Economic Report of the President, 1978*, p. 198.

[6] See *The Economist*, October 28, 1978, p. 97; and *Wall Street Journal*, November 1, 1978, p. 48.

[7] See *New York Times*, July 18, 1978, p. D-12.

[8] See Robert L. Heilbroner, *Beyond Boom and Crash*, Norton, 1978.

VI.

International Trade, Aid, and the "Weakness" of the Dollar

Whereas international trade had shrunk to a mere trickle during the Great Depression as a result of "beggar-thy-neighbor" policies and protectionism, there was a remarkable upsurge of foreign trade during the postwar years. As mentioned in the previous chapter in connection with agricultural problems, U.S. postwar policymakers took the lead in pushing for fewer import restrictions or controls and for freely convertible currencies.

Immediately after the war, there was a so-called "dollar gap," or inability of other countries to earn the foreign exchange necessary for the purchase of U.S. goods. Under these circumstances, loans (for example, the British loan of 1946), grants (the Marshall Plan and Truman's "Point Four Program," the predecessor of the various subsequent foreign aid programs), and the encouragement of the expansion of U.S. corporations into multinational activity allowed for the rapid rebuilding of Western Europe. At the same time, these activities contributed to the avoidance of serious recession at home, which most Keynesians had anticipated. The destruction of capital goods and factories in Western Europe and Japan during the war, and the politically determined inflow of labor from Eastern Europe and Asia, created something resembling nineteenth-century factor proportions and profit rates, thereby serving to revitalize the postwar capitalist system.

Top new monetary institutions responsible for setting the postwar "rules of the game" came out of the Bretton Woods Conference in 1944, which was dominated by the thinking of Lord Keynes: the International Monetary Fund (IMF) and the

International Bank for Reconstruction and Development (World Bank). A third proposed organization, the International Trade Organization, never got off the drawing boards, although this gap was eventually filled by GATT (the advanced capitalist club) and UNCTAD (the underdeveloped countries' club). The IMF was responsible for supervising so-called fixed rates of exchange between different capitalist currencies. As a result, there were only minor fluctuations in some exchange rates for many years. It was argued at the time that the fixed exchange rates reduced risk and thereby promoted world trade.

Occasionally, if a country had higher-than-average inflation, it would supposedly price itself out of world markets. The country in this position was said to have a balance-of-payments crisis. In such cases, the country could then get permission from the IMF to devalue its currency in relation to other currencies, which meant that there would be significant changes in the currency ratios for the country devaluing—a worsening of its terms of trade.

Ordinarily, large countries, such as Great Britain or France, devalued first and then notified the IMF, while underdeveloped countries had to seek the Fund's permission to devalue. If permission was granted, there were frequently strings attached, such as a requirement to cut back on government expenditures or otherwise to pursue austere monetary policies. If temporary factors (such as a crop failure) were responsible for the crisis, the IMF would supply a loan of foreign currencies to permit the country in question to cover its debts in the short run without a devaluation.

In contrast to these short-term loans, long-term developmental loans for power stations, transportation networks, and other infrastructural projects were financed by the World Bank. In addition to the principal loans, which charged commercial rates of interest, there was eventually a poor country window, the International Development Association (IDA), which gave long-term loans at low interest rates comparable to those dispensed by the USSR. In recent years the World Bank, under the leadership of Robert McNamara, has been pushing population control as an important solution to the developmental problems of the Third World.

As a result of these post war policies, there was a remarkable expansion of world trade, increased international division of labor, and significant positive "propensities to trade."[1] In some cases, such as the European Economic Community (EEC), a regional free-trade area or common market (similar to that existing within the United States) was designed to supervise and encourage greater specialization and trade. The idea of a Western European Common Market (only formally realized in 1957) seems to have been imported from the United States during the period of the Marshall Plan and the development of the European Iron and Steel Community, an early attempt to rationalize the production of iron and steel in Western Europe. In the same connection, it may be significant that when Great Britain decided to join the Common Market in the seventies—contrary to the wishes of the majority of the British populace, according to public opinion polls—President Nixon promptly congratulated the British government on its unpopular decision.

Common markets have also been attempted in Africa and in Latin America, but with little success. As a general rule, such associations have been comprised of economies producing essentially the same range of products, whereas the purpose of a common market should be to increase internal division of labor. Unless there is some planning mechanism—such as the Eastern European Council for Mutual Economic Assistance (CMEA)—with the power to direct this specialization, the prospects for common market development do not appear any brighter than those for single market development under capitalism.

In addition to rapidly expanding trade, a new Keynesian postwar institution, foreign aid, gained a foothold in the advanced capitalist world. When foreign aid is granted, instead of a two-way or balanced flow of goods and services, there is a one-way flow, presumably from the more developed or more affluent to the less developed or less affluent. This was in contrast to classical imperialism, which supposedly tended to produce the opposite effect. In the United States, foreign aid was frequently a tool of the Cold War since surplus military equipment could thus be transferred to countries of the "free world" along with capital goods for industrialization purposes. But comparatively neutral countries such as Canada and Sweden developed similar programs, frankly advertising the fact that jobs would be created in the process.

There was something of a political problem associated with the expansion of postwar foreign-aid programs in the United States. Because the domestic poor and middle classes felt that they should have greater access to aid, authorities tended to understate the magnitude of the foreign aid program. The figure usually publicized covers new appropriations only, while actual shipments have grown in a secular fashion. The Administration's proposal is frequently on the high side so that congressmen can reduce it and boast to their constituents that they cut back on foreign aid. The most recent new appropriation amounts to $9 billion, a postwar record, and we can be sure that the actual shipments will exceed this.

In the sixties, the dollar gap was transformed into a dollar glut, and the United States suffered a so-called balance-of-payments problem. Given the presence of a million "permanent tourists" stationed throughout the free world along with their dependents, the ability of the United States to export more than it imported, including goods and services consumed abroad, was steadily weakened. In addition, Western Europe and Japan recovered from their postwar shortages and became more interested in exporting their own surplus products.

The reaction in the United States was to resort to petty restrictions on free trade. Foreign aid was henceforth to be "tied" —that is, the underdeveloped country could only purchase products made in the United States. Tourists from the United States were limited in the amount of products that could be brought back into the country without paying a duty. Eventually, the Johnson Administration attempted to put limitations on our foreign investment in a vain attempt to preserve the former chronic export surplus. In some cases—for example, Western European cheese and Japanese textiles—quotas were designed to limit imports.

It became the conventional view that the United States was being priced out of world markets, and that the dollar was overvalued. There was, however, little statistical evidence to support this position. National Bureau of Economic Research studies in the early seventies and an article in the *Monthly Labor Review* in August 1971—the same month that Nixon announced his "New Economic Policy"—showed that unit labor costs since 1960 had risen less rapidly in the United States than elsewhere. While labor-productivity increases may have been less in the United States, particularly after 1966, the wage increases were also smaller here than elsewhere.

As will be explained in the next lecture (VII), I feel that the so-called devaluation of the dollar which began in August 1971 was designed primarily to get the U.S. economy moving again after the Nixon recession of 1969-71. It should be emphasized that the devaluation was only partial, since most countries in the world simply devalued along with the dollar (even socialist Yugoslavia took this action). The countries that revalued in relationship to the dollar were chiefly in Western Europe and Japan. The latter was at first reluctant to revalue and required a little arm-twisting before the Smithsonian Agreement in December 1971. The socialist countries (other than Yugoslavia), which have absolutely no aversion to improving their terms of trade via revaluation, and which have no interest in creating employment and growth through an export surplus, revalued with enthusiasm, much to the disadvantage of U.S. tourists and diplomats in these countries.[2]

The period of floating exchange rates was inaugurated by Nixon's New Economic Policy. It represents a victory for economists of the New Right, who assured U.S. policy makers that floating exchange rates would eliminate the balance-of-payments problems caused by fixed rates. Although governments have still intervened at times to produce a "dirty float," in general it has been the currency speculators who have determined the daily values of the principal capitalist currencies. As in any market, there are many opportunities for windfall profits to be made by selling dollars and buying stronger currencies and gold, as long as the dollar continues to depreciate. There is some evidence that U.S. multinationals and other banks, such as Franklin National, Citibank, Morgan Guaranty, and Chase Manhattan, have been engaging in such practices, contributing to the weakening of the dollar.[3]

Since 1971, the dollar has weakened in comparison to the

Japanese yen, the West German mark, and the Swiss franc, but there have been many devaluations or depreciations of other currencies in relationship to the dollar (Canadian dollar, Mexican peso, Australian and New Zealand pounds, all Scandinavian currencies, British pound, and Italian lira). Thus, when one takes a trade-weighted value of the dollar with respect to 46 other currencies, there has been very little overall weakening of the dollar.[4]

To some extent, U.S. officials such as Secretary of the Treasury Blumenthal have actually welcomed or issued benign statements concerning the weakening of the dollar in relationship to the yen, the Deutsche Mark, and the Swiss franc, since this has permitted U.S. products to compete more easily with products from these countries. The other side of this coin is the fact that the Japanese, West German, and Swiss businessmen have cried out for relief as a result of the constant appreciation of their currencies. And both Japan and the Federal Republic of Germany have sent their guest workers, including women, home.

One would have thought that the role of the IMF would have been weakened by the movement from fixed to fluctuating exchange rates, since the original *raison d'etre* of this organization was no longer valid. Nothing could be further from the truth, since now even advanced capitalist countries are coming under "exchange-rate surveillance" by the IMF. Thus, when Italy and Great Britain recently had to obtain loans from the IMF, they had to submit to austerity measures similar to those imposed on the underdeveloped countries all through the postwar years.

The oil-producing Arab states have also improved their terms of trade with the United States and the advanced capitalist system as a result of the OPEC agreement. While this jacking-up of oil prices in late 1973 is sometimes blamed for the growing U.S. import surplus, the fact is that our trade accounts showed about a $10 billion surplus as late as 1975—well after OPEC. The success of their agreement has whetted the appetite of other raw material producers to form similar cartels and to push within UNCTAD for a New International Economic Order for underdeveloped countries generally.

More recently, there seems to be a movement back toward fixed exchange rates in Western Europe, in the form of the European Monetary System (EMS), resulting from the Bremen Conference and originally scheduled to be inaugurated January 1, 1979. Henceforth, the West European currencies will have a comparatively fixed relationship with one another and will float as a unit against the dollar. This has understandably created some uneasiness in the United States, which still holds that the money markets can be relied upon to determine the relative values of currencies. There is also the fear that the IMF, which is dominated by the United States, will lose some power over "exchange-rate surveillance" in Western Europe.

President Carter's bold currency-support plan of November 1978, is designed to stop the steady depreciation of the dollar in relationship to the other strongest Western currencies, relying on the conventional belief that higher interest rates and tighter monetary policy can pacify the monetary speculators. In addition, there will be a loan from the IMF (presumably without austerity requirements), sales of paper and real gold, added swap lines, and securities dominated in the harder currencies, such as the Deutsche Mark.

As mentioned earlier, the role of the multinational corporation has increased greatly in the postwar years. U.S. tax laws intelligently discriminate in favor of their foreign activities, which relieve the capital surplus within the home country. In the immediate postwar years the multinational corporation played a major role in exporting capital to rebuild Western Europe. As the rates of profit have fallen in this area, however, there is now greater interest in capitalist exports to southern underdeveloped countries, as evidenced by the final statement of the Bonn Conference.

The activities of the multinational corporation are under attack, both in the Third World and in the U.S. labor movement. The Third World countries accuse multinationals of importing the wrong (capital-intensive) technology and of repatriating too large a percent of the surplus generated by their activities. Actually, since rates of profit should be higher in Third World countries (before discounting for risk), there may be some incentive to plow-back abroad rather than bring capital home where returns are lower. The U.S. labor movement assumes that these activities "export jobs" and would like them to invest at home as an alternative.

In my own view, the role of the U.S. multinationals—with some exceptions, such as ITT in Chile and elsewhere—has possibly been more positive than negative in its effects. While this may not be the *best* means to industrialize a country, it seems at least to be "workable," judging by the experience of countries such as South Korea, Taiwan, and Brazil. With respect to domestic employment, there is no evidence that investment at home is a viable alternative to investment abroad, since the profit rate is generally lower at home. And there is also the possibility that we may have seen the end of the postwar free-trade era and may be headed for an era of protectionism, in which case the overseas operations of the multinational corporation would be less vulnerable to a possible breakdown of free trade.[5]

At any rate, the machinery installed in our overseas plants is made in the United States by American workers and serviced by technicians and with parts of U.S. origin. On balance, the multinational corporation would seem to represent an employment-creating institution both at home and abroad, and one that tends to reduce the technological gap between the rich and the poor, and helps relieve the chronic domestic capital surplus and reduce the tendency for lower domestic profit rates.

Conventional classical and neoclassical economics maintains that imports are the fruits or objects of international trade. If the United States could solve its domestic underutilization problem using a bold Keynesian fiscal policy, as well as by demonetizing the system, this position might be safely taken. However, in practice, there is a tendency to rely on the neomercantilist export surplus as a creator of jobs—in itself an irrational goal. For, as Adam Smith pointed out, jobs are only a means to a rational end—the production of useful consumers goods and services.

Trade with the Soviet Union and other noncapitalist countries could permit a chronic export surplus if Soviet gold were used to balance the accounts. However, the official U.S. position is one of phasing out gold and substituting paper gold (Special Drawing Rights or SDRs) issued by the IMF. My own feeling is that the United States has perhaps reached a "mature creditor status" and should therefore welcome an import surplus, just as Great Britain did before World War II. If demand-pull inflation is a problem, this import surplus should increase domestic supplies and thereby reduce inflationary pressures. With foreign investments now exceeding the $100 billion mark, the profit repatriations and servicing of the debt should more than match any trade deficit.

Q. *Isn't there a contradiction between nationalism and the multinational corporation?*

A. I think you're right that there is a contradiction between the two, and to some extent this is reduced by the multinational corporations' being forced to hire executives from the country in which they operate. In other words, the nationalist sentiment has forced the multinational corporations to make concessions in terms of developing a local elite to help administer the branch in that particular country. If there were some harm being caused by the multinationals, obviously there would be a certain schizophrenia on the part of the local national working for the multinational. He would be somehow hurting his nation by working for the multinational. But I would argue that this is not so, that the multinational corporation is on balance a plus for the nationalist country, and I don't see why a national in an executive job should not work wholeheartedly for the multinational since it is helping his own country. It is only if there were harm being caused that there would be a contradiction.

Q. *Do you sincerely believe the multinationals are doing no harm? That is difficult to believe.*

A. Obviously there are differences among the multinationals. ITT has certainly earned its bad reputation. But remember that some of the multinationals have home offices in countries that are really nonhegemonic—Canada or Holland.

Q. *People like George Ball have argued that the nation-state is obsolete and its place is being taken by the multinationals.*

A. I'm afraid that's wishful thinking on his part. I think that the nation-state is going to be around for a long time.

Q. *Is there a contradiction between the Seven Sisters and OPEC?*

A. I don't think so. If you look at the profits of the Seven Sisters, they increased tremendously as a result of OPEC.

Q. *What about U.S. copper interests in Chile? Are the multinationals and the various nations in which they operate in harmony?*

A. Well, I think they will attempt to develop raw materials cartels similar to OPEC. They see the success of OPEC and they would like to imitate it. But I would say that it's very difficult to do this. In this respect, this is one of the very few things on which I agree with Friedman. I think history shows that cartels tend to break down, and I think even OPEC will eventually break down. It's already showing a great deal of weakness in terms of price shading. There's a great deal of price shading today in oil. I think that cartels are very unstable. I think the attempts to cartelize will be there, but I would say that they will be unsuccessful, unless you get the UNCTAD idea of the 17 commodities being organized with buffer stocks, etc. Something of an international nature coming out of UNCTAD might succeed, but I don't see private corporations being able to emulate OPEC.

Q. *What about the technology being supplied by the multinationals to the underdeveloped countries. Is it inappropriate?*

A. I think that the technological gap is closing as a result of the multinationals. If you look at the recent years, the underdeveloped countries are growing faster than the overdeveloped capitalist countries. This is the case in the last five years. I would say the multinational corporation has helped to close the gap. After the war, obviously, the United States accelerated the development of Western Europe. That period is over now, and so they're looking south to the underdeveloped countries as an outlet for surplus capital. I think we can see the same phenomenon in the United States. After World War II, there was a tremendous gap between the industrial North and the less-industrialized South. You had capital flowing as corporations were setting up operations in the South, so now you have a very small gap. The North has been rather stagnant, and the so-called "Sun Belt" has been growing very rapidly. So you had a closing of the gap as a result of capital flow.

The northern corporations relocated in the South, where they have so-called "Right to Work" laws, which means you can't easily have unions. Cheaper labor has produced more rapid growth in the underdeveloped South. If the underdeveloped countries had sound fiscal policies and full employment, they wouldn't have to opt for labor-intensive technology.

Q. *Why haven't you mentioned the role of multinational financial institutions?*

A. I don't consider them very progressive. I think that the banking community in general is sabotaging the advanced capitalist system. I don't see any difference between the IMF and National City Bank or any of the private multinational banks. It seems to me that the same mentality, the same ideology, the same pre-Keynesian ideology, dominates all monetary institutions, whether they be government or private.

Q. *Do you think there is a "Chinese Wall" between banking multinationals and industrial multinationals?*

A. I think that the industrial multinationals have internal reserves that they reinvest; in other words, they plow pack their profits. So the banking multinational is really in a different league. Perhaps small corporations will borrow from private international bankers, but the industrial multinational is as independent of the financial multinational as it is internally. In the United States 60 percent of all investment is financed internally, outside the banking system. The banking system does not finance most investment.

NOTES

[1] The propensity to trade measures the growth of foreign trade in comparison to the growth of global product in a year. Thus, a propensity to trade of 2.0 indicates that foreign trade is growing twice as fast as gross domestic product.

[2] Despite the revaluation of the Eastern European currencies, the dollar remains very strong in the black market. See my "Letter from Eastern Europe" *Challenge*, July-August, 1979.

[3] See "U.S. Probes Banks' Actions Involving Trading in Dollars," *Wall Street Journal*, November 2, 1978, for reports of foreign-exchange trading profits. Citicorps, for example, reported that this type of income rose from $54 million to $62.5 million, an increase that one analyst called "probably the biggest rise for any bank in any quarter."

[4] See *Fortune*, February 13, 1978, p. 71.

[5] In this connection, see my "The End of the Free Trade Era?" *ASTE Bulletin*, Fall/Winter, 1977.

VII.

Explanations of Inflation

There was a time when inflation could be explained entirely as a demand-pull phenomenon.[1] It was simply a question of too much purchasing power, or too much money in circulation, in relation to the existing or potential supply of goods and services. This was ordinarily the situation during wartime, when the demands of the military sector bid away resources from the non-military sector. Until World War II and its aftermath such inflations were ordinarily followed by deflation and relative price stability. As a result, there didn't seem to be any secular or long-term trend in price levels.

The U.S. economy after World War I illustrates this tendency nicely. The wartime demand-pull inflation was followed by a sharp deflation of prices in the 1920-21 postwar recession, followed by gently declining price levels for the remainder of the decade. During the early years of the Great Depression, the price level declined sharply by about one-third, and the price level on the eve of World War II was only slightly higher than it had been at the turn of the century.

This simplified view of inflation as a demand-pull phenomenon is still held by the Friedmanites and monetarists who see the "easy money" policies of the Federal Reserve Board as the root of the inflation problem. These pre-Keynesians or New Rightists see no trade-off between unemployment and inflation, and their Phillips curve is therefore vertical. Whatever the existing rate of unemployment, it can somehow be defined as "full employment." Thus, when the unemployment rate officially reached about 9 percent in the Great Recession of 1974-75, it was still considered to be full employment; the increase in the unemployment rate could be explained away by too generous unemployment compensation or welfare programs or by minimum-wage legislation, which had priced less-productive people out of the labor market. When prices rise, according to this school of thought, the Federal Reserve must take steps to "cool off an overheated economy." The price of money, or interest rate, must rise in order to reduce the demand for money and slow down investment and/or consumption. There is a further monetarist rationale for higher interest rates if the economy is also running a balance-of-payments deficit, as it was in the fall of 1978 when double-digit nominal interest rates became the rule.

It took some time for post-Keynesian economists to develop a different position on inflation. For one thing, there was no independent monetary policy until after the Treasury Accord of March 1951. Thus, real interest rates were for the most part negative during the Truman years. Then too, prices actually fell slightly in the 1949 recession, just as they might have been expected to do. The outbreak of the Korean conflict in June 1950 produced a speculative wartime surge in prices which was followed by price controls for the duration of the conflict. In his first campaign for the presidency, General Eisenhower in November 1952 promised to go to Korea to make peace and to get rid of price controls. To almost everyone's astonishment, when he fulfilled his promises, prices didn't rise but actually fell a bit. The Korean price-control system—unlike World War II price controls—had not really been controlling prices after all.

In the fifties, the conventional view was still that all inflation was demand-pull and that there was no such thing as cost-push inflation. Nevertheless, prices continued to rise in the Eisenhower years, despite the fact that there was obviously no excess demand for goods and services in the system. Capacity-utilization rates fell steadily from 1955 on until the Kennedy "New Economists" took the helm in 1961. In fact, during the second Eisenhower recession of 1958, when unemployment for the year officially rose to 6.8 percent, the President went on television to plead with American consumers to go out and buy more cars. (Unfortunately, this was the year of the Edsel.) His plea fell on deaf ears. The eight years of Eisenhower's relaxed economic policy proved that prices could continue to rise even though there was no evidence of too much purchasing power chasing too few goods.

Finally, establishment economists' views changed to reflect reality, and it was admitted that you could have cost-push inflation that was distinct from demand-pull. While the two types of inflation were independent phenomena, however, they supposedly worked in the same direction. Thus, cost-push inflation (which at that time was still used interchangeably with the term "wage-push" inflation) and demand-pull inflation simply reinforced each other. Wages rose and prices rose, and then wages rose again in an unending spiral, sometimes referred to as the "ratchet effect."

The "New Economists" of the Kennedy years came up with wage-price guidelines—which had already been explored by the British post-Keynesians—in an attempt to control wages and prices in the oligopolistic sectors. Beginning in early 1962, organized labor agreed to informal guidelines under which money or nominal wages were to rise by no more than 3.2 percent annually—a figure which supposedly corresponded with the historic increases in labor productivity. Industries capable of showing labor productivity gains exceeding 3.2 percent were supposed to lower prices, while those where labor productivity increases were less than 3.2 percent were allowed to raise their prices. But the effect of these guidelines on the price level was expected to be overall price stability, since unit labor costs would theoretically be constant.

These guidelines seemed to be effectively controlling inflation until 1966. But by this time it had become clear to organized labor that they had been sold a bill of goods. Under the Kennedy-Johnson guidelines, income going to profits had risen while the share going to wages had fallen. As a result of union leaders' demands for equity, money wages have increased since 1966 by at least 6 percent per annum, with the exception of the brief experience with wage and price controls under Nixon's New Economic Policy beginning on August 15, 1971, to be discussed shortly.

But, more important from the standpoint of controlling inflation, 1966 also represents a watershed marking the end of the period when labor productivity was rising rapidly (at one point by 3.8 percent per annum over a five-year period). Since that time, labor-productivity increases have been averaging at most 2 percent yearly, and the increases (and even decreases) have been extremely erratic. The only really healthy increases in labor productivity occurred in 1972 and 1975-76, when the economy was coming out of the two Nixon recessions. With money wages rising by at least 6 percent and labor productivity growing by under 2 percent annually, the average increase in unit labor costs has been at least 4 percent per annum over the period since 1966.

During the entire period, something developed which Arthur Okun has labeled a "bipartisan consensus." Instead of a vertical Phillips curve, as assumed by the pre-Keynesiàns, both Republicans and Democrats rallied around a supposedly negatively sloping Phillips curve. It was (and is) assumed that the rate of inflation accelerates as the economy moves back toward full employment. While both Republicans and Democrats have acted on this belief, the two parties have different priorities with respect to the relative importance of the inflation and unemployment problems. The Republicans ordinarily put a higher priority on fighting inflation, while the Democrats generally consider unemployment to be the more pressing problem. Thus, the Republicans allow the economy to recede further and further within its production-possibilities curve in a vain attempt to control inflation. The Democrats, on the other hand, are more inclined to stimulate employment, either by increasing defense expenditures or through such employment-creating programs as CETA, or both. The result of these differences in emphases is something I have already described as "political business cycles."[2]

Mention should also be made of the wage-price guidelines enacted by President Nixon in August 1971 and of the rationale for these controls, which were obviously inconsistent with the Republicans' ideology and certainly with that of the presidential advisers who were put in charge of administering them. Following a three-month wage-and-price freeze, new wage-price guidelines were introduced. But instead of promising price stability à la Kennedy, President Nixon's guidelines promised only a price level increase of 2.5 percent per year. Wages would be permitted to rise by 5.5 percent (instead of the 6 percent which had been a reality since 1966) and, again assuming an historic 3 percent increase in labor productivity, unit labor costs—and presumably prices—would rise by 2.5 percent yearly.

The Nixon wage- and price-control decision puzzled both his supporters (Friedman) and critics (Galbraith). We might attempt to solve this mystery. If we look at the U.S. economy during the first seven months of 1971, we see two important characteristics: (1) the rate of inflation had peaked in December 1970, and was coming down; and (2) the rate of economic growth was especially sluggish for a period when the economy was supposedly coming out of a recession. Thus, in my view, the wage-and-price controls were necessitated by the inflation the Nixon advisers anticipated (on the basis of the conservative conventional wisdom) as a result of the devaluation of the dollar, which was forced on such countries as Japan and the Federal Republic of Germany. The initial unwillingness of Japan to accept a revaluation of the yen was followed by a temporary 10 percent surcharge on Japanese exports to the United States. This surcharge was lifted only after the Smithsonian Agreement in December of the same year resulted in a complete Japanese capitulation on this score. The strategy worked beautifully, at least in the short run. The devaluation stimulated the U.S. economy to such an extent that labor productivity rose rapidly, profits were buoyant, and real wages—which had stagnated since 1966—even increased in 1972, all of which contributed to the reelection of Richard Nixon by a wide margin in November of that year.

The real inflationary impact of the devaluation was disguised for some time by the wage-and-price freeze and subsequently by the wage-and-price guidelines. The Nixon Administration eventually phased out these controls in four stages, and the true impact of the devaluation was felt in the "inflationary bubble" of 1974, when controls were abandoned altogether. Although the

OPEC Agreement is often blamed for the double-digit inflation of 1974, the principal culprit, in my view, is the cumulative, delayed impact of the devaluation of the dollar in 1971.

The Carter Administration is on the verge of announcing a third version of voluntary wage-and-price guidelines, one that will attempt to deescalate the basic inflation rate that in the first two years of the Administration seems to be averaging at least 6 percent. President Carter has attempted to set an example by holding wage increases of government employees to 5.5 percent, and it is being hinted that acceptable wage increases will henceforth be limited to the previous year's inflation rate. The effect of the decontrol of certain government price regulations on air fares is also being emulated in other areas. As a result of some deregulation and increased competition in air fares, there has been a significant reduction in the price of many fares, an increase in air travel, and in the short run, even greater profits for carriers.

The Carter Administration is also operating under the assumption that there is a relationship between deficit financing and the basic inflation rate. The problem with this approach is that it (1) overestimates the magnitude of the overall deficit; and (2) assumes the inflationary impact of what are still essentially "passive deficits." While the federal budget has been showing very large deficits—in the neighborhood of $50 billion yearly —state and local budgets have been running unprecedented surpluses. Their aggregate surpluses have been exceeding $30 billion, while the high-employment budget surplus for 1977 would have been $42.5 billion.[3] The budget deficits of the past decade have been essentially passive, that is, they come from the underutilization of labor and capital and the resulting decline in tax revenues rather than from significant increases in spending. Unemployed labor and capital do not contribute to government tax revenues and therefore produce massive passive deficits.

As mentioned in Lecture III, the first example of a significant passive budget deficit occurred in Eisenhower's second recession of 1958, when declining tax collections produced a $13 billion deficit—at that time the largest deficit since World War II. It is interesting to note that this passive deficit was larger than the active budget deficits during the Korean conflict. The important thing to realize, however, is that the huge passive deficit was followed by a period of very mild inflation. It is imperative to realize that active deficits produce demand-pull inflation, but that passive budget deficits associated with cost-push inflation are relatively noninflationary in the conventional sense.

The Carter Administration's pragmatic approach to the inflation problem includes a passive acceptance of the fact that interest rates must rise, although both President Carter and [former] Federal Reserve Board Chairman William Miller are clearly uncomfortable with this development. Here the roots of our own economic malpractice are much deeper. They stem from the Treasury Accord of 1951. In the following decade the Federal Reserve, under the leadership of William McChesney Martin, virtually stopped the growth of the real money supply in the process of resuming conventional monetary policy. While increases in the money supply have been more generous in the past decade, at least in nominal terms, the main source of cost-push inflation would appear to be too little money rather than too much.

Left-wing critics of capitalism tend to single out "profit-push inflation" or increased defense spending as explanations for the inflation of the seventies, but there is little statistical support for either hypothesis. In fact, real profits excluding petroleum since 1974 have been on the weak side since 1966, and defense expenditures in real terms actually declined when inflation was heating up during the Nixon years, as explained in Lecture II.

My own hypothesis is that secular inflation in the advanced capitalist system is rooted in the bloating of the service sector, which functions as a stabilizer for the system, albeit with certain costs—namely, sluggish labor productivity and a failure of the system to fulfill its tremendous potential emanating from rapid technological change.[4] The overdeveloped capitalist system would seem to be suffering from developmental problems related to the tendency for the rate of profit to fall, a characteristic that one of your intellectual ancestors had the genius to perceive.

To get the economic policy of the United States back on

the right track will require a truly herculean effort:

(1) A recognition of the fact that demand-pull and cost-push inflation are separate phenomena and ordinarily inversely related. However, the tendency for demand-pull and cost-push inflation to offset each other disappears after a devaluation. The devaluation makes exports cheaper, and the sudden foreign demand adds to demand pull. At the same time it also makes imports dearer, adding to cost-push inflation. The reduction in foreign competition also may allow for more administrative price setting. We can now see the new rationale for the conservative conventional wisdom that devaluations are highly inflationary and must be accompanied by austerity measures, particularly if the country is less developed and can cut back government projects. In the case of the United States, a price freeze and the Nixon guidelines were considered more appropriate for a major power fighting a losing war.

As the late Sir Roy Harrod once wrote, "the cure for each type of inflation is a little more of the other." My own Phillips curve is roughly horizontal (indicating about the same inflation rate) over a wide range of different rates of unemployment. But it reflects primarily demand-pull inflation at 4 percent unemployment, and cost-push inflation at 8 percent unemployment. In between, the demand-pull/cost-push "see-saw" operates to produce relatively constant increases in prices.

(2) A recognition of the fact that the U.S. economy has been experiencing basically cost-push inflation for the past decade, even during most of the Vietnam War. In this respect the Vietnam War inflation reflected a situation very different from that of either World War II or Korea.

(3) A realization of the fact that both Republican and Democratic Administrations have been prescribing demand-pull remedies for what has been essentially a cost-push situation. The most flagrant example of this economic malpractice occurred in September 1974, when President Ford called a summit conference of economists in Washington to build support for an increase in taxes to "whip inflation now." At the time, there was already a huge fiscal drag or surplus at full employment and the Great Recession had been well underway for the past nine months.

(4) A realization of the fact that cost-push inflation, or what is now more correctly called seller's inflation, is associated with passive government deficits, tight money policies and high interest rates, sluggish labor and capital productivity (sluggish capacity utilization rates), low profits, reduced defense spending, and rapid growth in the service sector outside government. Demand-pull inflation, on the other hand, is pretty much the opposite. It is associated with active budget deficits, easy money policy, rapid increases in labor and capital productivity, high profits, increased defense spending, and a slower growth of the service sector outside government. The real trade-off is thus not between inflation and unemployment. It is between demand-pull inflation at full employment and cost-push inflation and growing unemployment. And recent evidence would indicate that the rate of inflation would be lower if we had demand pull as its source.

(5) And, finally, a recognition of the fact that Sumner Slichter was right in the early fifties when he intuitively perceived that inflation was inevitable and functional in the advanced capitalist system. What he was unable to say, however, was that it preferably should be of the demand-pull rather than the current cost-push variety.

Q. *Why is inflation functional and what is the desired rate of inflation in the West and particularly in the United States?*

A. I think that inflation is functional in the advanced capitalist system mainly because it stimulates the propensity to consume and discourages the propensity to save. That is why inflation is functional. The rate of profit is related to how much demand you have in the system. If demand is buoyant, profits are going to be buoyant, and so the purpose of inflation is to stimulate consumption and to discourage saving. Obviously the desired rate of inflation is as low as possible. It's psychologically not very good to have 20 percent inflation in an overdeveloped country. Brazil can get away with 20 percent inflation, but in the United States it would be unthinkable. I doubt that we will even have double-digit inflation for extended periods. The reason we have inflation now is because the Carter Administration is telling farmers not to grow grain. It's the food prices, plus medicine, that are the basic source of inflation. The leading element in the cost-of-living index is medicine. It has been since 1966. Medicare has increased the cost of medical services very rapidly.

There is one capitalist country that has gotten rid of inflation completely. That's Switzerland. Switzerland has no inflation, or virtually none. But the cost is enormous. The declining industrial production in Switzerland in 1974-75, in the Great Recession, was one of the greatest, so they had to send their guest workers home. The Swiss have controlled inflation, but they have the potential for unemployment that they solved by sending their guest workers home and letting their own workers fill the jobs. I would say that the low rate of inflation in Switzerland, West Germany, and Japan is a sign of weakness, a sign of weakness in the labor market that has been solved by sending guest workers, including women, home. Japan and West Germany are the two advanced capitalist countries where the female labor-participation rate is falling—the only two. So the labor market is extremely weak in both these countries. They are the weakest of the advanced capitalist countries. It is no accident that these three countries are the countries where the bankers are in control. They have no fiscal policy to speak of. These are the countries that had fiscal policy before World War II, when they had very weak monetary policy. As a result of their defeat, they went in the opposite direction, restoring monetary policy, getting rid of fiscal policy, and adopting what we might call a completely free-market ideology. This is where the free-market ideology is the strongest.

Q. *Do you think that the low rate of inflation in Switzerland and West Germany is a sign of weakness in comparison with the United States?*

A. Women have been forced in Japan to give up their jobs for men. All these countries are using their foreign trade sector to solve their problems. They're dumping their surplus products on the world markets. Their export surpluses are a sign of weakness, not a sign of strength.

Q. *Aren't Japan and West Germany growing?*

A. This comes from the export sector. It's not coming from domestic production, it's coming from the export surplus. The use of the export sector to get growth is a sign of weakness. And the Soviet

Union is providing the mechanism for West Germany to solve its problems. The West Germans run an export surplus with the Soviet Union and the Eastern bloc generally. In this way, they are maintaining their growth. It's a short-term measure. It can't continue. They're really skating on very thin ice.

Q. *And if we in the Soviet Union have balanced trade with West Germany, then what?*

A. They would be in much more trouble, obviously. The West Germans on the surface look as good as they do because of the Soviet Union.

Q. *I can't understand why in principle a balance-of-trade surplus is a sign of a weak economy.*

A. It's only if you're neomercantilist that it can be considered positive. You have to be irrational to think that an export surplus is positive, because the fruits of trade are the imports and the costs are the exports. If you put international trade on an input-output relationship, the input is the export, and the output is the import. If you exaggerate or emphasize the cost instead of the benefit, you are behaving very irrationally. It's only the socialist countries that behave rationally in terms of trade. When they trade, they ordinarily look first at what they want to import, not what they export. They are nonmercantilist.

Q. *If internal demand is satisfied and we are able to produce in excess of that demand and make a profit, why is it a cost?*

A. Profits are properly a goal of individuals and corporations but not of governments or societies as a whole. The object of the economics game, according to Adam Smith, was the production of useful goods or services. They can either be produced internally or produced abroad and imported.

Q. *Can you account for the growth of monopoly during the last recession, and isn't that producing limits on competition?*

A. I don't think there has been a significant increase in monopoly, mainly because the most rapidly growing sector is the service sector. The service sector is very competitive, and it happens to be the main source of cost-push inflation. The service sector continues to grow in a recession. As a matter of fact, it tends to grow faster during a recession. It's the sluggish productivity in the service sector, caused by the crowding of potentially unemployed people into the service sector, that brings about the rise in prices.

Q. *But you said that it was farmers' not growing grain that was responsible for inflation.*

A. Actually, both are responsible, and so are high interest rates and rising unit overhead costs.

Q. *Do you have more inflation with more competition?*

A. The oligopolies have had less inflation than the service sector, and the key is productivity. Productivity rises in oligopolies and is much more sluggish in the service sector. And so it's not the monopoly or oligopoly that creates inflation; it's the service sector. And if you have to look at productivity, the key thing to look at is both labor and capital productivity. Take banking, for instance. Banking is a service. We have added a tremendous amount of computerization to our banking, and yet our productivity in banking hasn't increased at all, despite the increase in computers. And the reason is that we waste the potential to improve productivity in having a hundred different varieties of checkbooks, a great amount of nonprice competition. We give away free consumer goods for opening up new accounts—a gigantic waste of resources by the banking business. That's one example of a part of the service sector that has the potential to increase productivity but is wasting it.

Q. *Why should banks not want to improve productivity? And how are they different from industry, which also engages in nonprice competition, sometimes with a loss of profit?*

A. Banks are very competitive but engage in a tremendous amount of nonprice competition. In this respect, they resemble the monopolistically competitive firms rather than the oligopolies.

Q. *How does crowding come into the picture?*

A. The crowding effect into services is found chiefly in the distribution process and the development of new services—consultants of all kinds, for example, It is difficult to make a move now without consulting someone—a psychiatrist, an expert on summer camps for children, a tax accountant, a lawn doctor, etc.

Q. *What is the main factor responsible for inflation?*

A. The service sector. The reason for its growth is more complicated. It is related to the development problems of the advanced capitalist system.

Q. *Why is long-term inflation confined to the post–World War II years?*

A. I think the key factor here is the Keynesian Revolution. It committed the advanced capitalist system to something resembling full employment. And that really is the heart of why we have inflation now and we didn't have it in the nineteenth century and even after World War I. As I mentioned before, the price level in 1940 was no higher than it was in 1900. So something happened as a result of World War II, and I would argue that it is the Keynesian Revolution—committing us to full employment and resulting in a very active labor market, which permits us to increase money wages faster than the increase in productivity. And so one underlying factor is sluggish productivity as the basis for the rise in unit labor cost. I do not blame wages for rising unit labor costs; I blame productivity. That's why you can't really compare it to the nineteenth century. The key turn of events was that we cannot afford to have another Great Depression, in part because of the socialist challenge to capitalism. In the Great Depression, the price level fell by one-third. But for political reasons we're now competing with a system that has full employment, relatively steady growth, and no inflation problem or balance-of-payments problem. And so we have to behave differently in this world where we're competing peacefully with another system.

Before World War II we obviously didn't have that need to create full employment. You Soviets were not really competing with us in the 1930s. You were going through a tremendous industrialization drive. The standard of living didn't increase at all in the 1930s, in contrast to the postwar period, wherein the standard of living has been rising from 3 to 5 percent per year. So it's obvious that we didn't have to have full employment before World War II. The Keynesian Revolution gave us the theory to guarantee something resembling full employment. Now in the course of time the monetary authorities have gradually weakened our commitment to full employment. And these monetary authorities are especially strong in Switzerland, West Germany, and Japan. If we continue to follow the influence of the monetary authorities in these three countries, we will get falling prices, we will get a Great Depression. I don't think we're that stupid, but it is a possibility.

NOTES

[1] This lecture was given before the Political Economy Kafedra of Moscow State University on October 11, 1978.

[2] In his original use of the term "political business cycles" in 1943, Michal Kalecki assumed wage-push inflation at full employment since he made no distinction between wage-push and cost-push inflation and took no account of the different rates of change in labor productivity at different levels of capacity utilization.

[3] These huge surpluses, which exceeded $6 billion in California, encouraged the development of a "Proposition 13" mentality.

[4] In this connection, see my forthcoming article "Trends in the Economic Systems of the World and the Growth of Services."

VIII.

Monetary versus Fiscal Policy

According to the bipartisan consensus economists, monetary and fiscal policies are complementary tools to be used in guiding the advanced capitalist system along a path of steady growth. The problem, in a nutshell, is to find the proper combination or "mix" of the two types of policy, emanating respectively from the Federal Reserve Board and the Treasury or Office of Management and Budget.

In actual practice, however, there has been a great deal of "leaning against the wind" since the Federal Reserve regained its power following the Treasury Accord of 1951. If fiscal policies became expansionary, the Federal Reserve Board considered it advisable to tighten up on monetary policy. On the other hand, if the budget became tighter, the Board would presumably *consider* easing up on monetary tightness.[1] In other words, each policy tended to offset or neutralize the effects of the other.

Generally speaking, the two political parties have displayed different preferences when it comes to the use of monetary and fiscal policy. The Republicans, who have pre-Keynesian tendencies, are more inclined to prefer the use of monetary policy, particularly the tightening thereof to control inflation. The Democrats, on the other hand, are prone to use fiscal policy—specifically the increase in defense expenditures or the introduction of the investment tax credit—to create jobs. As explained earlier, this has produced something I have described as postwar political business cycles.

From a theoretical standpoint we might consider four possible combinations of monetary and fiscal policy, the latter two of which would constitute "leaning against the wind."

(1) Both monetary and fiscal policy could be easy. This would involve low interest rates and deficits in the high-employment budget. This is the typical combination to be found in wartime when the security of the state is at stake, e.g., during World War II. At this time, the principles of "sound public finance" were considered less important than the defeat of Hitler.

(2) At the other extreme in the array of policies, both monetary and fiscal policies could be tight. In such cases we would find high interest rates accompanied by a surplus in the high-employment budget. Such a combination of monetary and fiscal policies existed at the time of the economic summit called by President Ford in September 1974.

(3) Or we might have an easy monetary policy in combination with a tight fiscal policy—a leaning against the wind. Here, low interest rates would be combined with a surplus in the high-employment budget. This is the combination preferred by Paul Samuelson, since it would presumably result in a higher rate of investment and growth, supposedly with a damper on inflation.

(4) Finally, we might have a tight monetary policy combined with an easy fiscal policy. This means that high interest rates could be found alongside a deficit in the high-employment budget. John Bunting, one of the very few Keynesian bankers, might be found advocating this combination.

While most advanced capitalist countries follow policies combining various mixes of monetary and fiscal policy, it is possible to have an economy run with primary emphasis on monetary policy and with very few possibilities for the employment of the budget to affect economic activity. Most of the states that had been fascist during the thirties adopted (or were forced to adopt) such a policy after World War II. Since the fascist governments had largely demonetized their economies to the extent that they had only minimally independent monetary policy, there was a sharp backlash in the other direction after the fascists were defeated. In Spain, where the fascists survived the war, the demonetization continued roughly until the late fifties.

In the Federal Republic of Germany, the postwar model was referred to as a "social market economy," with bankers simply adjusting interest rates in an effort to steer the economy in the proper direction. Should the economy become overheated, interest rates would be raised; should it become stagnant or sluggish, interest rates would be lowered. It wasn't until the 1966/67 recession in West Germany that fiscal policy began to come back to the Federal Republic, and even today it is fair to say that West German bankers are still pretty much in the commanding heights. This is one important reason why the world's monetary speculators—including U.S. multinational banks—intuitively feel that the Deutsche Mark is sound.

Monetary policy was the preferred tool of the pre-Keynesians. Fiscal policy was favored by the mature Keynes, although his earlier *Treatise on Money* is still respected by the New Right. In *The General Theory* there are very few references to the use of monetary policy, despite the fact that it appeared six years after the *Treatise*. In one instance, Keynes cryptically called for a lowering of interest rates to deal with an overheated economy —something that was not of practical interest during the sluggish, underheated thirties.

Hitler was the first practicing "Keynesian"—some years before *The General Theory* appeared in print. The same ideas had already appeared in the writings of Kalecki, in Polish. It is just possible that some of Hitler's economic advisers were aware of Kalecki's work. And, since Jews were prominent in the Weimar Republic's banking community, Hitler was able to use his anti-Semitic ideology as a means to divide German monetarists.

While Hilferding and Schacht were calling for a devaluation of the Mark to price German products back into world markets —in line with the typical capitalist beggar-thy-neighbor policies of the time—Hitler held firm to the existing high value of the Mark and introduced exchange controls to ration or change the product mix of imports, much as the Soviet Union did after the Revolution. By 1936, when the German economy had gotten back to full employment, it became something of a suction economy, tending to import more than it exported. It may also be significant in this connection that the Germans under Hitler were uninterested in regaining as markets the underdeveloped African parts of the German Empire, which had been lost at Versailles after World War I.

Keynes recognized the value of his *General Theory* to Hitler. In his September 1936 introduction to the German edition, Keynes wrote that the Germans must be "thirsty" for a theory that would explain the rationale for what they were already doing with great aplomb. In Keynes' words:

> How hungry and thirsty German economists must feel after having lived all these years without [a theory]. Certainly it is worthwhile for me to make the attempt. And if I can contribute some stray morsels towards the preparation by German economists of a full repast of theory designed to meet specifically German conditions, I shall be content.

Keynes felt that his new ideas were more easily adapted to the conditions of the totalitarian state than to England, and this was one of the reasons why he referred to his paradigm as a "general" theory.

The primary employment of monetary policy can also have some impact on the growth of monopoly power. Since the large corporations tend to finance their investment chiefly out of internal reserves, it is primarily small businesses that are adversely affected by rising interest rates designed to cool off an overheated economy.

As mentioned above, all advanced capitalist countries tend to subsidize agriculture. They tend to subsidize industry as well. For this reason, the typical advanced capitalist country can now be referred to as a "subsidy state." Industrial subsidies tend to take the form of rapid depreciation allowances and, in the United States, the relatively unique investment tax credit.

The investment tax credit was initiated by President Kennedy in 1962 as a tool of the New Economics in reducing fiscal drag. By allowing a 7 percent rebate on the cost of new equipment invested during the past year, the Kennedy Administration was able to cut the taxes collected from industry and to increase internal investment reserves. The investment tax credit was briefly abandoned for four months at the end of 1966, as explained earlier, and again at the beginning of the Nixon Administration, but was resuscitated by Nixon's New Economic Policy. At present, it seems to be institutionalized at 10 percent rather than the original 7 percent, and there is even talk of a "refundable" investment tax credit by Senators Long and Kennedy.[2]

Accelerated depreciation allowances produce the same effect and have long since been institutionalized in most advanced capitalist countries. By artificially exaggerating depreciation, the corporation can maximize paper costs and thus reduce its corporate profits tax payments. Such devices are part of the so-called tax expenditure budget, which totaled $134 billion in 1978.

Artificial stimulants to investment produce good short-term results, as evidenced by the investment binge occurring from 1962 to 1966. But unless such a policy is accompanied by some sort of plan to redistribute income, it simply creates a huge realization problem with excess capacity—a capital hangover—in relationship to consumer demand. In their effect, the Kennedy-Johnson tax policies were roughly comparable to the "trickle-down" philosophy of Republicans since Herbert Hoover.

In a certain sense, the New Economics of the Kennedy-Johnson years produced a realization problem similar to that brought about by the relatively free market conditions of the 1920s. The only difference between the end of the two periods was that there was no defense spending to speak of in 1929, while there was the Vietnam War in the late sixties. As the Vietnam War wound down, however, the underlying structural weakness of the advanced capitalist system became more obvious.

Ever since Tugan-Baranowsky, at least, there have been economists who have argued that there is no necessary connection between investment and consumption under capitalism. Presumably one could continue investing in new capacity and more productive technology without worrying about whether or not there was sufficient purchasing power to keep the new productive capacity working. There is an obvious relationship between this idea and Say's Law.

The Stalinist economic policy carried out in the thirties in the USSR did prove that Tugan-Baranowsky and others could be right under certain circumstances, but these circumstances were hardly representative of the capitalist system. At times, Paul Samuelson has held that there is no reason why the advanced capitalist system couldn't emulate the Soviet economy and continue investing at high rates without regard to the income distribution.

In my opinion, however, a tax policy producing greater income equality is complementary to a tax policy artificially stimulating investment and new productive capacity. Without this complement, there will simply be additional requirements for unproductive or "certified" consumers and waste institutions generally.

The following question is frequently raised: Why should bankers behave in a way that is antithetical to the best interests of the system? Bankers are very much like any seller under capitalism: they try to get the highest price possible for the item they have to sell—money.

They are also reluctant to reduce the price of money. They prefer to substitute nonprice competition, for which U.S. bankers are justly famous.[3] In addition, they have a special dislike of inflation, which is used as a justification for increasing interest rates. They are the only group that must legally hold money in a sterile form (reserves), so inflation naturally erodes their real assets.

There is also some evidence that the profits of banks tend to rise during the recessions that their policies help bring about, since industrial profits are weaker and internal reserves smaller during recessions. Thus, the necessity to resort to bank borrowing increases during a recession, bringing with it increased profits for the banking community. In other words, bankers are no different from other economic interest groups: they place self-interest above the needs of society as a whole.

Q. *Which of the four possible combinations of monetary and fiscal policy do you prefer?*

A. The first.

Q. *Who is John Bunting?*

A. John Bunting is the President of the First Pennsylvania Bank in Philadelphia and the author of a book entitled *The Hidden Face of Free Enterprise*, one of the best books I've seen. He has a chapter on monetary policy entitled "That Old Black Magic."

Q. *Did* The General Theory *completely eclipse the* Treatise on Money*?*

A. Yes. It's interesting that Friedman likes the *Treatise* very much.

Q. *Just what is the tax expenditure budget?*

A. You're spending taxes that could be collected when you give corporations something like the investment tax credit, and so Congress has forced the Administration every year to list the so-called tax expenditure budget in addition to the regular budget. Congressmen thought that the loopholes were somehow getting out of control, and they wanted to monitor the size of these loopholes. Actually it's a subsidy, but they don't like to call it that. They want to disguise the fact that they're subsidizing corporations. In effect, they are interest-free loans. This allows for the growth of internal reserves as a source of investment.

Q. *What does the term "trickle-down" mean?*

A. Trickle-down is a term that we use to describe the preference for investment over consumption. Obviously it's a little bit related to Stalin's policy in the 1930s, or "supply side" economics.

Q. *Is the banking system completely a waste institution?*

A. Obviously, any economic system has to have banks, but I think of money as a liquid that makes the wheels turn, and to a great extent capitalist banking is, as Bunting said, "old black magic"; that is, there is a lot of mystique attached to what covers up a comparatively simple operation. So I would say that socialist banking is on the right track. I always judge socialist countries on what kind of banks they have. If they have nice old banks in old buildings, that's a good sign. If they have very modern banks with abstract paintings on the walls, that is not so good. Yugoslavia has beautiful banks with air-conditioning and beautiful pictures on the walls, plus high interest rates, and is an example of a rather corrupt socialist economy. The Yugoslav economy pretends to be socialist, but has all the basic negative characteristics of a capitalist economy.

Q. *But the interest rate doesn't depend on the pictures on the walls. I think we should have low interest rates and modern buildings.*

A.   Actually, high interest rates are all right for the Soviet Union. If you have a capital shortage, this should be reflected in the interest rate. One of the reasons that you have been rather wasteful in the use of working capital is because the interest rate is too low. With a low interest rate, you don't economize on working capital. So I would say that the two systems should exchange levels of interest rates.

Q.   *What is the difference between working capital and banking capital?*

A.   The enterprise gets its working capital from banks. In other words, if the manager of an enterprise can't pay his wage bill, he uses his credit, that is, he has to go to the bank and borrow temporarily in order to pay his workers. Or if he has too much inventory ... You keep too much inventory in parts of your economy precisely because you have such low interest rates on working capital. It's something like 1.5 to 2 percent. Obviously you don't think about it, since it's such a small percent. If you had 7 or 9 percent, you would economize on inventory and generally on working capital.

Q.   *What is your attitude toward the so-called dual banking system in the Soviet Union, where one part is the construction bank, and one part is the Gosbank?*

A.   Actually, you have had a number of changes over the years, and I'm not sure what the current situation is. Do you go to a separate bank for new construction? As you know, at one time you had an agricultural bank. You have a history of a number of specialized banks in addition to Gosbank. I think that probably the main function of Gosbank is to act in the same fashion as what we call the GAO, the General Accounting Office. They check the returns of enterprises to make sure that nobody is cheating the state. The Gosbank is important, but it's not nearly as important as our bank. Our Federal Reserve bank is very powerful. You don't really have monetary policy.

Q.   *Why do banks try to eliminate small businesses?*

A.   It's not that they consciously try to eliminate small business. It's just that when they raise interest rates, it only affects the small businessman—and the economy. The large corporation isn't affected at all, because generally speaking they don't borrow.

Q.   *Why is this?*

A. I think that they roll their own. The margin between price and cost is such that they have a lot of internal financing. Sixty percent of all investment comes out of the margin between price and cost. And their costs are as low as they are because their productivity increases are higher than in the other sectors.

Q. *Is there a conflict between managerial people and the stockholders of large corporations?*

A. Every manager in the United States tries to pay out as little in dividends as possible, and to plow back as much as possible. His job depends on the growth of the corporation. And the corporation grows by reinvesting surplus value. You pay out as little as possible of surplus value in dividends and plow back as much as possible. The only conflict occurs at the annual stockholders' meeting. You always have a few little stockholders who complain that their dividends are not high enough. But they are not very significant. The manager determines his own salary in accordance with the size of the firm. So in general there is a conflict between the recipients of dividends and the management.

Q. *In America, aren't the penalties for not paying taxes about 6 percent?*

A. It's actually gone up a little bit. I just paid a penalty myself. My tax accountant made a mistake, and the State of New York sent me a bill for $1,300 and included in that bill was $170 interest. I filed my return in April, and I got this bill six months later: that's a rather substantial rate of interest. I don't know, but the corporate rate may be different. The tax laws are all rigged for the corporation and against the individual. After all, who makes laws in Congress? They are not ordinary people. You couldn't get elected to our Congress if you were a worker at this time. Some time ago we wanted to find workers in our Congress, and I think they found six people who had worked manually at some time in their lives . . . and one of these was a bartender! The people in Congress reflect business by and large, and so the tax laws are made for business. They're not made for workers or for ordinary people. If you're a businessman, it's a lovely system. In the Soviet Union, if you're a worker, it's a pretty good system, but if you wanted to be a businessman, you'd say it's a lousy system.

Q. *But there are no businessmen in the Soviet Union.*

A.   Oh yes there are. I met some on the black market. [Laughter.] These are frustrated businessmen. In our country they would be presidents of corporations. That's the kind of mentality it takes to be successful under capitalism. If you can make windfall gains by buying something cheap and selling it at a very high price, obviously you can get rich very fast. That's the whole difference between the systems. You think that's a crime, but we reward somebody who does that.

Q.   *What is the purpose of nonprice competition in the service sector?*

A.   It's the same reason that we have nonprice competition in the industrial sector. Price cutting can be dangerous for any seller. It can lead to a price war. One of the ways that sellers learn to live with other sellers is to compete with advertising or nonprice competition. It does come out of profits, but it is still better than a price war which might eliminate profits altogether.

Q.   *How do banks attract savings?*

A.   As I said, with things like this [pointing to tape recorder]. Actually, it's not only that. After all, you get income in your pay check, and you want to put it in a savings account. Which savings account do you put it in? So it's not just transfers, it's also new saving that is attracted like this, or is attracted by the fact that you have air conditioning, that you have original paintings on the walls, etc. There are different types of banks, but there is one thing they all have in common. If you drive across the country and you come to a small town, the best building in the town will be the bank. And the best house in the town will belong to the banker.

Q.   *Do you really think that Hitler's government policy was Keynesian, or was it just a joke? I read John Kenneth Galbraith and he proclaimed that the first Keynesian was Hitler, but the thing is that Keynes left the institutional system of enterprises intact, and Hitler did quite the opposite.*

A.   Why do you say that Hitler did the opposite? After all, private capital was still intact. Profits were still intact. Personal profits were still being made under fascism.

Q.   *But there was a greater degree of nationalization.*

A. Not any more than you have in the advanced capitalist system. Look at France or Italy or England, where you have a tremendous amount of nationalization. Nationalization does not mean socialism. It just means that sector of the economy had a falling rate of profit, and the private sector doesn't want it any longer, so they turn it over to the state.

Q. *Haven't advanced capitalist countries nationalized their defense industries?*

A. Not in the United States. Wherever you have a high rate of profit, you don't ordinarily get any nationalization. There have been people, such as Galbraith, who wanted to nationalize defense, but he's the only person I ever heard of who advocated that. I would be very surprised if England and France had nationalized their defense. I think that profit is still important there too. Why else would they want to sell to China and other countries? The British are selling some very advanced military equipment to China.

NOTES

[1] Because of the overriding fear of inflation, there has been a bias towards leaning in one direction—undoing the effects of expansionary fiscal policy.

[2] The "refundable" investment tax credit would permit checks to be drawn on the Treasury to make up for the difference between the investment tax credit for the year and the calculated corporate profits tax whenever the former exceeded the latter.

[3] The production of checkbooks in hundreds of different varieties and the distribution of a large array of consumer goods to those who open new accounts illustrate this phenomenon. The proliferation of branches has also been remarkable in recent years, thereby stimulating the instances of bank robberies, particularly in New York City.

IX.

The Growth of the Service Sector and the Distribution of Income: A Symbiotic Relationship?

Orthodox economists believe that the growth of the service sector in the advanced capitalist system reflects consumers' higher income elasticity of demand for services. In accordance with Engel's Laws, Colin Clark and others have long noted an apparent tendency for economic development to proceed in three stages: agriculture, manufacturing, and finally, as we all become more affluent, a shift toward services.

However, specialists on developing countries, such as Gunnar Myrdal, have also noted that the service sector in underdeveloped countries (India, for example) is frequently bloated with urban refugees from the countryside. It is my belief that the overdeveloped countries have a tendency to develop a similar bloating of their service sectors. Thus, the growth of the "service glut" tends to stem from the supply side rather than the demand side of the labor market. It is an outstanding example of the Galbraithian "revised sequence" or dependence effect.

It is also assumed by economists such as Victor Fuchs that there is something inherent about the service sector that results in smaller increases in labor productivity as compared with the nonservice sectors. The argument is that the opportunities for applying capital in the service sector are fewer than they are elsewhere. The result is that the increases in labor productivity in the service sector have recently been about half as great as the gains in the nonservice sectors. Thus, the more rapid growth in the labor force employed in services is assumed to stem from some inherent differential in the ability to increase labor productivity. Resources are *pulled* into the service sector, according to Fuchs, rather than *pushed* or crowded there as I assume. Obviously, both interpretations are closely related to the nature of contemporary inflation. If we are operating in a cost-push environment, as I have assumed, it makes greater sense to believe that resources are pushed into services.

Comparisons of the growth of the service sectors in the advanced capitalist and the advanced socialist economies throw some light on the question of the laws of motion underlying the development of services in the two types of systems. From the beginning of planning, the Soviet and Eastern European service sectors have exhibited certain "laws of uneven development" in relationship to earlier capitalist economic history. The state planners have put a higher priority on the development of transportation and communications, medicine, education and culture than is usually found in capitalist service development. On the other hand, in comparison with capitalism, there has been a relatively sluggish growth of personal services, housing, advertising, installment credit, banking, and insurance in the advanced socialist system.[1]

Beginning in the late fifties and early sixties, the Soviets finally began to place a higher priority on the development of personal services, and are still doing so. In 1978, the volume of services increased by 7.7 percent, while retail trade grew by only 4.5 percent. In the 1979 annual plan, the goals for the growth of household services (7.7 percent) considerably exceed the goals for the growth of objects of consumption (5.4 percent).[2]

While both advanced capitalist and advanced socialist economies are developing their services at a more rapid rate in recent years, there is apparently one significant difference between the two developments. Under the advanced socialist system, the increases in labor productivity in the service sector are not too different from those taking place in the nonservice sectors. To some extent, this difference between the two systems may reflect longer *ocheredy* or queues in the Soviet Union (and thus be at the expense of consumers' productive use of time), as well as the overcoming of a certain initial backwardness in the services (such as the *kassa* system) through the rapid expansion of self-service. But it does seem that the tightness of the labor market may also be a factor encouraging greater mechanization and efficiency in the supply of services in the advanced socialist system.

Because of the sluggish growth of labor productivity in the service sector in the advanced capitalist system and the fact that wage increases in these sectors—especially the wages of government employees, who have increasingly become unionized —have been about the same as they have been elsewhere in the economy, the unit labor costs here have been rising much faster than they have in the nonservice sectors. Thus, there is a good underlying basis for the fact that the service component of the Bureau of Labor Statistics consumer price index ordinarily is in the vanguard with respect to inflation.

This has been particularly true with medicine, as well as banking, according to studies conducted by the Bureau of Labor Statistics. Despite the many possible applications of computers and other productivity-increasing technology in both areas, the data indicate that the changes in labor productivity in both sectors are minimal, and very possibly negative. To the extent that the demand curves for both services are highly inelastic with respect to price, the higher unit labor costs are readily passed along to consumers. This is particularly true with respect to medicine, where the introduction of Medicare and Medicaid in 1966 created great inelasticity of demand with respect to price. If the government is going to pick up the tab, there is undoubtedly an incentive for sellers to take advantage of the situation.

The recent rapid growth of the U.S. labor force and labor participation rate, and especially the growth of employment in services, has certain demographic bases. Because of the postwar baby boom in most countries within the advanced capitalist system, there have been unusually large numbers of people in the cohorts entering the labor market or attempting to enter the labor market. The problem of youth unemployment is particularly acute in Western Europe and has resulted in a certain amount of alienation among the college-educated who are unable to utilize either their potential or their education. In the United States, young people have been meeting the challenge of finding employment by participating in the explosive growth of the service sector. Their self-employment frequently involves catering to those in the upper-income groups, whose demand for self-indulgent services is highly inelastic with respect to price.

The movement to protect the environment and to give consumers greater protection, as typified by Ralph Nader, has also been a source of employment for young idealists. Young persons from upper-income families have taken up these causes with great enthusiasm. Having become surfeited with the fruits of the advanced capitalist system, they frequently subscribe to a no-growth ideology. Thus, there is a certain amount of cooperation between the environmentalists and the conservative elements in society, neither group being particularly worried about further growth—although for different reasons. This uneasy alliance was most evident at the Ford summit meeting of economists in September 1974.

The environmental movement is sometimes blamed for the recent sluggishness in labor productivity. It is assumed that investment in pollution-control devices occurs at the expense of more productive types of investment. Since there is no apparent shortage of capital, this hypothesis seems weak. The environmental movement may have contributed to some cost-push inflation, but it is at least a healthy variety thereof—one that creates more jobs.[3]

Studies by John Kendrick assume that there will be some upturn in the rate of increase in labor productivity in the eighties, possibly as a reflection of the baby bust which began in the sixties, and the resulting smaller numbers of young people in the cohorts who will be entering the labor force. But at least one economist (E. F. Renshaw) has testified before the Joint Economic Committee to the effect that he foresees no further increases in labor productivity by the turn of the century.

A certain growth in the service sector is also related to the continued inequalities in income and wealth. Certainly the problem of youthful crime must be related to the life-styles of those with more income than they legitimately need, coupled with the frustration of not being able to find productive jobs. The whole business of crime and punishment and rehabilitation is one of the advanced capitalist system's most rapidly growing sectors.[4] The problem of narcotics addiction would also seem to be exacerbated by the failure to solve the unemployment problem. And the reformed addict can always be absorbed by the system of services as a consultant and/or therapist for those still addicted.

It is sometimes thought that the emphasis on affirmative action (for women and minorities) should have resulted in greater equality in income distribution. While there was some closing of the discrimination gap between white and black incomes during the sixties, when the New Economics was seemingly producing higher growth rates and fuller employment, the discrimination gap seems to have widened in the seventies. Black incomes have ordinarily been more equally distributed than white incomes, but this may be changing due to the new opportunities opened up for educated blacks.[5] Thus, black income distribution seems to be becoming more unequal, with upwardly mobile educated blacks receiving good incomes, and the black underclass sinking still further into the ghettos.

The growth of a Proposition 13 mentality threatens to widen still further the income differences between the rich and the poor. One of the means by which those in the lower income groups have tended to receive higher incomes is through increased local government expenditures, a fact recognized and publicized by Galbraith in the fifties, when he was advocating increased sales taxes.

The failure of the advanced capitalist system to move toward a more equal distribution of income (and the actual movement toward a more unequal distribution of wealth) would seem to be the heart of the problem—the conflict between productive potential and consumption. The resolution of this conflict can only be achieved by a shifting in the historic proportions of investment and consumption. Investment in greater productivity would appear to be futile and even wasteful as long as people with unsatisfied basic needs still do not have the wherewithal to keep the resulting new productive capacity operating at optimum rates for spreading overhead costs.

NOTES

[1] See B. Szabadi, "Performances of the Tertiary Sector in Hungary—an International Comparison," *Acta Oeconomica*, no. 2, 1977, pp. 167-82.

[2] *Pravda*, November 30, and December 1, 1978.

[3] The President's Council on Environmental Quality has calculated that the pollution-control industry now employs 400,000 workers, while 17,600 other employees lost their jobs when plants closed because of stricter controls. See *New York Times*, April 17, 1977, IV, 8E. The environmental movement—but not its no-growth aspects—would appear to be functional to the stabilization of the advanced capitalist system.

[4] To some extent, the rising crime rates have been the result of the baby boom after World War II, just as the present falling rates are the result of the subsequent baby bust.

[5] The Gini-coefficient for the nation as a whole is misleading as an indicator of the black income distribution. Since over half of the black population is found in the south, where Gini coefficients for the blacks and whites have been higher than they are in the rest of the country, the black Gini for the country as a whole is misleading. When looked at by regions, the black Ginis have ordinarily been lower than the white ones. See Sharon Oster, "Are Black Incomes More Unequally Distributed?" *American Economist*, Autumn 1970.

X.

Toward a Revisionist School of Economics?

As promised in the introductory lecture, now that we have come to the end of this series of lectures on the problems of the advanced capitalist system, I will summarize my general position and answer your initial question about the "school" to which I belong. My general position includes emphasis on the following points:

1) Defense expenditures have been basically positive or functional in the postwar years. They are endogenous to the system, and their fluctuations are related to the political party in the White House, thereby giving rise to the political business cycle.

2) The Vietnam War was the first war fought at less than full employment with basically cost-push inflation, passive deficits, low profits, and growing unemployment of capital and labor.

3) The United States is currently running a very high full-employment surplus if the budget at all three levels of government is taken into account. Attempts to reduce government spending in order to balance a budget that is running a passive deficit can only be counterproductive. Such a policy is the modern version of the "paradox of thrift."

4) Unit overhead costs (including interest charges) and sluggish labor productivity are the basic sources of cost-push inflation, which is unrelated to wage-push inflation, at least in the long run.

5) The advanced capitalist system is suffering from developmental problems related to the failure to adjust smoothly to

lower rates of return to capital; failure to move toward the euthanasia of the rentier and a more equal distribution of income; and the general inability to approach in a rational manner a no-growth economy, as foreseen by the nineteenth century political economist John Stuart Mill. The result might be labeled a "creeping realization problem."

6) The service sector is the main generator of secular inflation at the same time that it stabilizes the system with respect to employment. Thus, it is at the heart of the stagflation problem.

7) The whole postwar period can be analyzed as a struggle between monetary (pre-Keynesian) and nonmonetary (fiscal or post-Keynesian) policies, in which the former have gradually been winning out, to the detriment of future capitalist economic development. The weakness of the individual advanced capitalist economies is related to the acceptance of monetary or pre-Keynesian policies. Thus, Japan and the Federal Republic of Germany paradoxically are the weakest links in the system.

As to the school to which I belong, it should be obvious that it is to the left of the bipartisan consensus. Although I have friends in all three left-wing deviationist schools, I have certain reservations about each school.

1) The Galbraithians tend to deemphasize the role of maximizing profits; treat the United States economy in comparative isolation from the rest of the capitalist system; and subscribe too often to the convergence hypothesis. Galbraith himself is too rigid with respect to not cutting taxes and too anxious to impose price controls.

2) The New Left tends to be too cavalier about the unimportance of the division of labor and efficiency generally; tends to be too critical of the existing noncapitalist systems (with the exception of China); too critical of the multinationals; and not critical enough of the international monetary community.

3) The Old Left tends to be too cavalier about the development of nuclear power; too rigid about the role of the women's movement in the United States (i.e., opposes the Equal Rights Amendment); fails to take into account the contradictions within capital (industrial versus financial capital) and with-

in labor (the dual labor market); and is not critical enough about the noncapitalist system (with the exception of China) to to suit me.

Thus, I would prefer to describe myself as belonging to the Revisionist School—perhaps even its only member. It is revisionist in the same sense as our "school" of Revisionist Historians, who have sought to indict the United States policy makers for at least having complicity in the instigation of the Cold War.

Epilogue: Reactions Abroad and At Home

In addition to the nine lectures given at Moscow State University in Lenin Hills, I delivered lectures and/or had serious discussions at the Institute for the Study of the United States and Canada, the Institute of World Economy and World Politics, the Financial Institute of Moscow, the Leningrad Financial and Economic Institute named for Voznesensky, and the Latvian State University in Riga, before leaving the USSR. The lectures basically repeated the materials in the chapters on military spending, inflation, income distribution, and international trade, or varying combinations of these controversial subjects.

Most Soviet Marxists I encountered in Moscow favored monetarist explanations of inflation. One exception was Professor George Solyus of the Financial Institute, whom I had deliberately sought out since I was familiar with his writings on the subject. Solyus was aware of the slow growth of the money supply in the 1950s and thus favored a theory of inflation that traced rising prices to growing monopoly power. As in the United States, budget deficits and military spending were also frequently believed to be sources of inflation. Generally speaking, Soviet economists were unaware of the huge surpluses that had developed at the state and local level as a result of President Nixon's revenue-sharing plans.[1] My comparatively benign treatment of military spending in this regard was considered to be "unacceptable" and "super-academic" by the head of the economics division of the Institute for the Study of the United States and Canada, Yuri Bobrikov.

After leaving the Soviet Union, I spent over three months

traveling and lecturing in Europe, mostly before socialist audi-
ences, in the following institutions: Institute for the Study of
the Problems of Capitalism, Warsaw; Humboldt University, Ber-
lin; Institute for World Economics and Karl Marx University,
Budapest; the University of Venice; and the University of Biele-
feld in the Federal Republic of Germany. As in the USSR, my
position on the role of military spending and its relatively positive impact on the advanced capitalist system since World War II
created the greatest antagonism or controversy. Economists in
the German Democratic Republic were familiar with the hypothesis of Seymour Melman and the studies of the International
Association of Machinists to the effect that military spending
created fewer jobs than other types of government spending,
and my reactions to these ideas have been included in Lecture
II. My hypothesis that the two weakest links in the advanced
capitalist system are Japan and the Federal Republic of Germany
was also a bit hard for socialist economists to swallow since
they were usually impressed by the high level of Japanese and
West German technology, but the East Germans were especially
intrigued, if not encouraged, by this possibility. Hungarian and
Polish economists proved to be surprisingly neomercantilist, in
part due to their growing indebtedness to Western bankers. And
many Hungarian economists seemed to be looking forward to
partial convertibility of the forint as a possible solution to their
current difficulties.

Since my return to the United States, many people have
asked me what it is like to teach Soviet students. The answer in
a nutshell would have to be that it is not too different from
teaching economics at Hofstra University. As Marshall Goldman
has already revealed in a series of Op-Ed pieces in the *New York
Times* (January 25-27, 1978), Soviet students have been greatly
influenced by the writings of John Kenneth Galbraith. Since my
students were mostly graduate students specializing in the study
of the United States and Western Europe, they were extremely
well informed on the subjects of my lectures. They had read
most of the mainstream works of the Western economics establishment, and frequently expressed admiration for the high level
of our technology. Although official Soviet statements deny

any possibility of ideological coexistence in an era of détente, my experiences support the hypothesis that some convergence is actually taking place in the *thinking* of economists in the two worlds.[2] While some economists in the West have begun to take Marxist theories more seriously, the socialist economists at present seem comparatively uncritical of the writings of our traditional or bipartisan economists, such as Charles Hitch or Arthur Burns. Paul Samuelson's *Economics*, which was originally translated (badly, it turns out) in the early 1960s, is still highly regarded and serves as a key to understanding the capitalist system. After my first lecture, I learned from one of my students that there was much debate over whether or not I was really an economist, particularly since there was no evidence of mathematics in my presentation. Some of those who heard me were convinced that I was more of a sociologist or political scientist: Can it be that Marxism is more fruitful as a tool in the hands of dissenters than it is in the hands of an economics establishment such as in the USSR?

There were times when it appeared as if I were indeed skating on thin ice. This seemed to be the case whenever I found it necessary to bring some of Khrushchev's ideas or policies into a lecture or discussion. The reaction was invariably one of enigmatic smiles, if not titters. Evidently, the late Premier is not exactly the nonperson official Soviet texts would have you believe. My stock dropped to its nadir when I expressed the opinion that the space program in both the United States and the USSR was a huge waste of resources, given the real needs of this planet. My timing was particularly inappropriate since the Russians were about to welcome the return of their cosmonauts after 140 days in space. Serious Russian interest in outer space antedates the Revolution, and it seems clear that the space ventures have considerable popular support in the USSR.[3] My doubts about the safety of nuclear power plants were also apparently not shared by my audience. Although my students were very well informed with regard to the capitalist economies, there were certain lacunae in their knowledge of Soviet and Russian economic development. For example, none of my students was aware of the Stalinist bias toward a falling price level, particularly after 1947. While they were aware of the theories of Tugan-

Baranowsky, they were not quite sure of the meaning of a Potemkin Village. In all fairness, my students in the United States would have some trouble with these references too.

While I was in the USSR, the Romanian government announced its defection from the Warsaw Pact Nations' policy decision to increase military spending by 3 to 4 percent, in response to the NATO policy of increasing real defense expenditures by a similar magnitude.[4] At the same time, the official line at the Institute for the Study of the United States and Canada was still that the Soviet government had been constantly reducing military spending. Thus, when I brought up the Romanian deviation as evidence to the contrary, this naturally produced a certain amount of tension. Among the other Eastern European countries, only the German Democratic Republic seemed ready and willing to announce a 4 percent increase in military spending.

How can one account for the basic conservatism of Soviet and East European economists and students of economics when it comes to their analyses of the advanced capitalist system? It seems to me that there are at least three factors underlying their response to my lectures.

First, there is the virtually literal acceptance of Marx's ideas, which had greater relevance in analyzing nineteenth century capitalism than they do for the contemporary period. Marx, like other economists of his time, believed in a commodity theory of money. In his paradigm, there was a close connection between gold (or other precious metals, such as silver) and the money supply. It seemed obvious at that time that major gold discoveries were frequently followed by increases in general price levels. In the USSR there is a comparative absence of a creative Marxist tradition, such as that being slowly revived in the German Democratic Republic and Hungary. In the former country where Rosa Luxemburg has been rehabilitated into a national heroine, and where dialectical discussions within a Marxist-Leninist framework are more traditional, there would seem to be the seedlings of creative thinking on the subjects of inflation and capitalism generally.[5]

Second, there is an overall assumption that the U.S. economy must be operating on the same rational principles as the Soviet or Eastern European economy.[6] There has been a tendency for full employment and demand-pull inflation to be a permanent feature of the Soviet-type system, while cost-push inflation has been controlled by a strict incomes policy since World War II. Under such conditions, too much money or purchasing power in relationship to the potential supply of goods can be a very serious problem. Deficit financing in this overheated economy would be highly inflationary and it is for this reason that the typical noncapitalist government budget calls for a small surplus each year.[7] Likewise, increased military budgets—as projected by the Warsaw Pact decision in 1978—can only exacerbate the problem of repressing inflation.

Finally, all of the above is reinforced by the need of the Soviet and Eastern European economies for an environment of détente and the corresponding thinking that would strengthen this policy. The muting of criticism of the United States in general, and of the capitalist economy in particular, during the years since détente was proclaimed by Nixon and Brezhnev, is obvious. Our level of technology is rightfully respected in Eastern Europe and our *potential* output under conditions similar to their seller's market is most impressive. Thus, it is not too surprising that one of the most optimistic predictions on the future of the advanced capitalist system has come out of Hungary.[8]

In their own discussions and writings, Soviet and Eastern European economists seldom mention income distribution, despite the fact that most Western studies, including those of the World Bank, conclude that there is considerably greater equality in the income distribution of the noncapitalist world.[9] In fact, economists who were active in Prague's spring thaw in 1968 argued—along lines made famous by Arthur Okun—that greater inequality would increase the efficiency of the Czech economy. The Hungarian New Economic Reforms of 1968, which were similar to those being touted by the Czech economists of the time, have indeed produced somewhat greater inequality in the Hungarian income distribution. In much the same manner, market socialism has probably increased the inequality of incomes within Yugoslavia. It would seem that the greater the influence of market forces, the greater the possibility for those with more talent to reap rewards and those with less talent to fall behind.

Is it possible that greater inequality is relatively harmless (economically, if not ideologically) in the fully employed non-capitalist world at the same time that it is counterproductive in the advanced capitalist system? I would argue that this is the case. In fact, I made this point in one of my Moscow lectures when I suggested that the greatest return from East-West trade would be obtained as a result of an exchange of *levels* of interest rates in the two economies. For countries that have solved their macroeconomic or full-employment problems, greater efficiency may in fact take place as a result of greater material incentives and the ensuing greater inequality of income. On the other hand, countries that increasingly fail to solve their full-employment goals should work for greater income equality, both nationally and internationally.

Since returning to the United States, I have circulated my manuscript to a number of people for criticism and lectured on some of my revisionist ideas. One of my friendly critics (Robert Lekachman) felt that I was "too optimistic" about the economic condition of the United States; another (Ray Franklin) expressed the view that my criticism of the bipartisan consensus was "too cute." A questioner at Southern Oregon State College expressed the view that I had depicted "capitalism with an inhuman face." For the record, I should like to make it clear that I am not an admirer of Herbert Hoover, Adolph Hitler, or Richard Nixon. Nevertheless, no one is completely imperfect, and this applies to all three of these gentlemen. And I admit that I am optimistic enough to believe that the Proposition 13 mentality — as reflected in the Kemp-Roth bill and attempts to provide constitutional limits on government spending—as well as the coming to power of Margaret Thatcher in Great Britain, are not harbingers of things to come. Rather, these developments represent the ebb and flow of forces in a system that is in trouble and grasping for straws.

Neither am I in favor of increased military spending by the United States or the Soviet Union, as seems to be in the cards until the year 1985. As an alternative, I favor greater East-West trade, since there is a trade-off between these two roads. Although

I feel that the USSR had achieved rough military parity with the United States by the mid-seventies, I believe that the scenario for this development differs significantly from that claimed by the Central Intelligence Agency. Specifically, I suspect that Soviet defense expenditures before 1960 were much lower than our CIA estimates of the time, which frequently then assumed a parity of the two arms budgets.[10] Instead the Soviet Union was undoubtedly cutting corners on military spending and using a policy of extreme secrecy to cover their missile and other military gaps. As a result, Soviet overall economic growth rates were extremely rapid in the fifties, giving rise to Khrushchev's famous prediction that their economy would "bury" ours before too long.

Two things occurred in the sixties that forced the Russians to increase their real defense spending significantly, perhaps by as much as twofold as claimed by President Carter's 1978 speech at Wake Forest College in Winston-Salem, North Carolina. One was the Sino-Soviet split in the early sixties, which forced the deployment of a significant share of Soviet troops and equipment to the Chinese border. The other was the inability of the Russians to camouflage their real military weakness in the sixties with a continued policy of extreme secrecy. In effect, our spies-in-the-sky provided us with "inspection" and forced them to increase real defense spending and close the military gap in the sixties. At one point in mid-1961, Premier Khrushchev announced a midyear unprecedented 50 percent increase in their defense budget, partly as a reaction to his meeting with the newly elected President John Kennedy in Vienna. One result of these increased military expenditures was a marked slowing down of Soviet economic growth rates, especially in the early sixties.

Relatively small increases in Soviet military spending in the seventies—particularly in view of détente and the winding down of the Vietnam War—are largely conjectural and may be partly statistical in nature. Since the CIA now prefers to emphasize Soviet military spending by using a so-called dollar-weighting system, the ending of the draft in the United States produced a sudden statistical increase in Soviet defense spending, provided a later weighting system is used.[11] Since we were forced to pay much higher wages and salaries to a much smaller volunteer army after 1973, the use of the new higher U.S. pay scales to value or weight the roughly 4 million strong Soviet military forces probably produced a largely artificial increase in Soviet defense spending relative to the United States in the mid-seventies.[12]

In any event, it seems clear that projected increases in defense spending will have a different impact on the welfare emanating from the two systems—stimulating our overall growth and slowing down theirs.[13] While a similar stimulus to our growth could conceivably also emanate from greater East-West trade—in view of the lopsided relationship between exports and imports to and from the Soviet Union—this alternative would be positive for Soviet growth and welfare generally. It is for this reason that we may count on the Soviets to bend over backwards to continue the policy of détente begun during the Nixon Administration. By the same token, the United States can be expected to resist Soviet disarmament and arms control initiatives, just as it has all through the postwar period.[14]

The questions below were posed by Yuri Bobrikov, head of the economics division of the Institute for Study of the United States and Canada, following my lecture there.

Q. *I'd like you to elaborate on the recession in the United States in 1974-75. Why, in your opinion, did this recession take place after all the statements in the 1960s that you had gotten rid of recessions? I remember President Johnson's last* Economic Report of the President *in January 1969, when he said that you would never again let the economy go astray.*

My second question is related to your views on military spending, which seem to be too academic. You seem to put military spending on the same plane as regular factors. Military spending represents means of destruction which might be a tragedy for humanity. You spoke of these factors from a super-academic viewpoint. I would like to quote an article by Ann Crittenden on "Guns and Butter" in which she says that the Carter Administration is cutting nonmilitary programs in favor of military spending. I'd like to get your opinion on the present role of military spending in the United States.

Thirdly, would you comment on the anti-inflationary policy of the present Administration? Do you believe that the Carter guidelines contain the risk of recession?

A. Obviously I think it is very important to distinguish between pre-Keynesian and post-Keynesian thinking. I think the Republicans in general are the source of pre-Keynesian thinking and policies, and that the Democrats are the source of post-Keynesian thinking and policies. And so you've had since World War II eight years of expansion followed by eight years of relaxation, followed by eight years of expansion followed by eight years of relaxation. And now we have embarked on our third postwar expansion under the Democrats. So far it seems that Carter is behaving more like a Democrat than like a Republican. Defense spending has gone up as it had under previous Democratic administrations and I would say that this is one reason why the U.S. economy is doing as well as it is doing. The U.S. economy is the strongest of the advanced capitalist economies. If you look at the Western European capitalist economies, you will find that unemployment is still growing. The United States has the best recovery record from the Great Recession. And I would say that one of the engines of this recovery is the fact that Jerry Ford began the increase in defense spending and President Carter has continued this policy. I see no mystery why the U.S. economy is the strongest and has the best recovery since the Great Recession.

Why did we have the Great Recession? Obviously, I think it has something to do with attempting to apply a remedy for demand-pull inflation when in reality we had cost-push inflation. Essentially, we have had malpractice at the highest levels. Our economists have been practicing bad economics. They've been practicing an economics that simply will not work in the advanced capitalist system, one which is increasingly not working. So if you look at the Great Recession, you see that we were doing nothing to counteract it. As I pointed out, at the summit meeting of September 1974 Ford was actually advocating an increase in taxes at a time when the economy was already going downhill. It began going downhill in November 1973, and here you are in September 1974, talking about raising taxes to "whip inflation now." If you talk about raising taxes at a time when the Great Recession is just getting going, obviously something is wrong with economic policy. It's the most obvious example of horrendous economic policy. It wasn't until March 1975 that we finally passed a tax cut. By then the economy had already run downhill for a year and a quarter. So obviously we haven't been applying a policy that would be required to avoid a Great Recession.

I don't think the Nixon policy deserves all of the credit for the

Great Recession. It really began under Johnson. So I tend to talk about the bipartisan consensus of Arthur Okun, Johnson's economic adviser, and all of the Nixon advisers, such as Paul McCracken, the first Republican Chairman of the CEA. They all essentially interpreted the Vietnam War as a typical war during which you had demand-pull inflation. According to this view, you had to raise taxes to slow down the economy. If you look at what happened during the Vietnam War, it doesn't bear any resemblance to this. The amount of unemployment of capital began to grow after 1966 and continued to grow all through the Vietnam War. We never got back to full employment during the Vietnam War. If you look at the labor unemployment rate, you have something that looks like full employment but isn't. Because what happened was that all of the manpower-training programs under the Great Society Program of Johnson finally got going in the late sixties. You had people moving from one retraining program to another with no jobs at the end of the line. You had about 1 million people employed in manpower training if you take into account all of the administrators, all of the teachers, and all of the poor people who were being trained for jobs that didn't exist. The unemployment rate looked like full employment, but the real situation shows up in the capacity-utilization rate, which began to decline in 1967 and continued to decline all during the war. It's the only war in which we've had a mini-recession and a regular recession in the same war. Obviously it's a different type of war than either the Korean War or World War II. Unless you understand the difference between demand-pull and cost-push inflation you can't make correct economic policy. If you ask any administration economist what is the difference between the two, he or she will say there's no difference. They don't understand the offsetting effect of the two types of inflation.

We might compare the 1960s with the 1920s. In the 1920s we had a free-market economy. The role of government was zilch. There was no defense spending to speak of in the 1920s. We have the best example of a Friedmanian economy in the 1920s. What did this produce? It produced a huge realization problem. By 1929 the capacity to produce goods was so great in relation to the ability to absorb these potential goods that we had a huge realization problem. What happened in the 1960s was that the government planners created a huge realization problem. By instituting the investment tax credit, they created an investment binge and a tremendous amount of capacity to produce goods without anybody available to absorb the potential output of this capacity. So that we had a fantastic capacity to produce goods by 1966, without the ability to absorb them. Even with the Vietnam War, with increased military spending, we still didn't get back to full employment. If you want to know why the economy was as weak as it was during the Great Recession, it was because the Nixon Administration actually reduced real defense expenditures. One of the effects of this, which Nixon himself bragged about, was that we had his first recession in 1970-71. When we had this recession, Nixon said, "I planned it that way." He understood it, but the conventional economists didn't like it being said. He continued to reduce defense spending throughout his six years, so that when we get to 1974, we have only the stabilizing effect of military spending along with weakness in the economy.

The source of inflation is sluggish productivity showing up mainly in the service sector, the growth of which has been just about half of what it was in the nonservice sector.

Well, as far as looking into the future in my crystal ball is concerned, obviously we can have a recession if we continue to follow the pre-Keynesian policy. If we continue to raise interest rates in a futile attempt to cool off an overheated economy that isn't overheated, we are going to end up like Switzerland. If we continue to give in to the monetarists we will get no growth at all, no increase in wages, send guest workers (illegal aliens) home, push women back into the home. Fortunately we have a women's liberation movement which will probably resist rather than go back into the homes as during the 1930s.

I think it is important for Marxists to understand that the main contradiction now is not between labor and capital. This was true at one time, but at the present time the main contradiction under capitalism is within capital. It's between the monetary or financial capitalists and the industrial capitalists. The industrial capitalists are the good guys and the monetary economists are the bad guys, and they have very different interests. The monetary capitalists actually benefit from a recession. If you look at bank profits in a recession, they always go up. The reason they go up in a recession is that their business improves. When you have a prosperity, the large corporation doesn't have to go to the bank for funds since it plows back its internal reserves. The recession, which the banking community has planned, causes the bank profits to go up. The same thing shows up in the international sphere. In my view, the multinational corporation is a positive force. These are the good guys. The bad guys of course are the IMF, the source of all evil for the underdeveloped countries. It is only coming to the surface now, because in the past it only affected underdeveloped countries. Now it's beginning to affect overdeveloped countries. Italy and Great Britain recently had to submit to the same idiotic policies that the underdeveloped countries have been submitting to since World War II. So in my view, the IMF is the main source of the problem as far as the international community is concerned. The multinational corporation is by and large a positive force, spreading technology throughout the world. And I would make the same argument for defense. Research and development couldn't get through Congress unless it came under the aegis of the Department of Defense.

One of the main sources of technological change in the United States is the defense budget. As far as great destruction, you are right. If we have World War III we are all in trouble, but so far we have been sane enough to avoid it. As far as the U.S. is concerned, defense spending is very positive since it makes the capitalist system look as if it were working. The purpose of war is to destroy capital and to create high rates of return to capital. It restores nineteenth-century capital-labor relationships or proportions. There has been an equalization of rates of return to capital between the United States and Western Europe, so that now there is an incentive for capital to flow south where there is still a capital shortage.

Will the guidelines reduce inflation? The guidelines would be appropriate *if* we had demand-pull inflation. But the main thing to reduce the present inflation would be to stop the idiotic agricultural policy. We're telling our farmers not to grow so much grain. It's been very successful. The grain crop this year went down something like 8 percent. If you set-aside a lot of land not to grow grain, this is going to be an inflationary factor—this is going to keep agricultural prices higher than they otherwise would be. So I would say the set-asides in agriculture are the main source of food inflation certainly. Interest rates are another main source of inflation. You have to somehow control the monetary authorities before you can get rid of double-digit interest rates. Carter had appeared to be an easy money man, but you can see how weak he has been in terms of holding down interest rates. Even Federal Reserve Board Chairman Miller, who was an industrial capitalist, has had to go along with higher interest rates.

So I think we would be misleading ourselves if we didn't recognize the fact that the monetary, pre-Keynesian forces are still very strong and they are responsible for the double-digit interest rates. The belief that we have a balance-of-payments problem is one of the worst diagnoses possible. If we really have an inflation problem, we should welcome an import surplus. Carrying this thinking to its logical conclusion, having an import surplus is a good thing. It increases the supply of goods domestically. So there is absolutely no reason why the United States should worry about an import surplus. We should be the one country that plans to have an import surplus every year. There is no reason why the United States shouldn't adjust to the fact that we are a mature creditor, the same way that Britain was before World War II. We can live on our interest and profits repatriated from our foreign investments. We don't have to have an export surplus. We can afford an import surplus to control our domestic inflation. Worrying about a balance of payments is a sign of the corruptness of our policy—a sign of the continued and growing influence of our monetary economists, our pre-Keynesians.

There is one thing that Keynes tried to teach and that is to never worry about a balance-of-payments problem if it conflicts with domestic policy. So he helped devise fixed exchange rates at Bretton Woods. We had comparatively great success with these until 1971. One of the reasons we are in trouble now is the floating exchange rates. It's the worship of the market that is the source of the problem. We think somehow that if it's a market-determined price of foreign exchange, it's better than a fixed price. You don't have that hang-up. By and large you have fixed prices here and you don't have the market ideology. But if you begin to develop a market ideology as in Yugoslavia, you will have exactly the same problems as Yugoslavia. You can have the socialization of the means of production and have all of the same problems that you have under capitalism.

Q. *There are many things we could discuss, but we must discuss your ideas concerning military spending as an alleged factor in economic growth. I was, frankly speaking, confused by your presentation. We have had other American economists here, but I've never witnessed such a benevolent attitude toward military spending. If we follow this logic, that military spending produces growth, then war would be still better since it also increases demand. We cannot accept this kind of logic. I don't think that you really mean that.*

A. I mean it sincerely, that World War II saved the capitalist system for a period of time. If you look at the capitalist system before World War II, it was thoroughly corrupt. The Great Depression was the sign that capitalism was through, and World War II saved the system, destroying capital, restoring the rate of profit. And the Cold War did exactly the same thing. The rate of profit in defense is much higher than it is in nondefense.

Q. *So following this logic, World War III would do the same thing?*

A. No. World War III is unthinkable. Now that we have nuclear weapons, it is a different ball game.

Q. *There is no such thing as military spending in a vacuum. The logic of the arms race is unacceptable. In the long run, military spending means loss of GNP.*

A. From your standpoint, I can understand why you think the way you do. There are two possibilities for the advanced capitalist system. You have to admit the fact that capitalism exists, it has certain laws of motion, and that one of its laws is a falling rate of return to capital. You can have a Great Depression as in the thirties, or military spending. So you ask yourself, which is better? From the standpoint of a U.S. citizen, I don't think anyone would want to go back to the Great Depression. He still thinks he is better off with military spending than he would be with the Great Depression. Every worker knows that his job depends on military spending. Why do you think it was that there was only one vote against the neutron bomb? I would say that the worker is smarter than most economists. Why can't we do the cities over? What is there about spending for cities that is different from spending for military? We know what value is in housing, we know what value is in construction. We do not know what value is in a missile. So military cost accounts can be padded very easily. We can't make the profit on urban renewal that we can on missiles.

The problem is that you people are operating on your production-possibilities curve, and when you increase defense spending as you are planning to do in the Warsaw Pact countries, it is going to cut into your growth. We operate within our production-possibilities curve at all times, so we can have our cake and eat it too. The reason why we are not operating now at full employment is because we haven't changed the income distribution since World War II. If anything, the distribution of wealth is more unequal than it was 30 years ago. There has to be a fundamental redistribution of income, which is detrimental to the interests of the capitalists. We can't wish away this problem. You can't talk about getting rid of defense until you start redistributing income; that has to come first. As long as you have the advanced capitalist system, waste is functional. Once you understand this, everything falls into place. Military spending has one advantage relative to other waste: at least you get technological change, which you don't get out of the service sector. You as a country can use our technology, and thus you are benefiting from our defense budget through East-West trade.

There was a very interesting lead article recently in the London *Economist*, pointing out that the Western countries, including Britain, had an advantage over the Soviet Union. The Western countries could increase their defense spending and this would take up slack in the system. The socialist countries would be very hard pressed to meet this competition as compared with Britain, which has 6 or 7 percent unemployment. This is realism. You may not like it, but it is realism. You should ask yourself, What am I going to do when the capitalist countries increase their defense budgets by 3 percent in real terms? The answer is not to increase Warsaw Pact defense expenditures by a like amount. It seems to me that you are playing into the hands of the people who are ready, willing, and able to increase defense spending. If you're going to increase defense spending because we do, the escalation has begun again.

NOTES

[1] The Soviet budget is a consolidated budget consisting of expenditures and revenues at all levels of administration, and it was assumed that the U.S. budget was all-inclusive as well.

[2] See my "The Convergence Hypothesis: The Planning and Market Elements in the Development of Soviet, Western and Developing Economies," in Proceedings of National Association for Comparative Economics Meetings, San Francisco, California, December 27-29, 1966, pp. 63-67, for an earlier recognition of this phenomenon. This article is reprinted in Carlo Schneider, ed., *Convergenze tra Capitalismo e Socialismo*, Giuffre Editore, Milano, 1978, pp. 151-60.

[3] The same cannot be said for the other Eastern European countries. Representatives from these countries have been included in recent flights, but the local cosmonauts seem to be subject to a certain amount of derision.

[4] The Romanians reportedly transferred $41.5 million directly from its military budget to raise family allowances. The increases for NATO countries can be traced to an agreement in principle reached in 1977 and accepted in May 1978 by the leaders of member countries. Although the spending increases are subject to review every two years, the defense ministers of NATO countries (excluding France, Iceland, and Greece) at a recent meeting agreed to an annual increase in real expenditures of 3 percent through 1985. See Drew Middleton, "NATO Extends 3% Rise in Annual Spending to '85," *The New York Times*, May 16, 1979, p. A9.

[5] In Czechoslovakia, I was informed that their books in political economy do not cite East German sources since they are considered to be too revisionist. In Hungary, two of their leading economists have discovered the paradigm of the Polish revisionist Marxist, Kalecki, and are doing serious research on the economy using his framework. Mention should also be made of Rudolf Bahro's *The Alternative in Eastern Europe*, Schocken Books, New York, 1978.

[6] My Soviet translator, for example, had some difficulty with the concept of the real interest rate. This is quite understandable since in the USSR there has been virtually no difference between the nominal and real interest rates for the past 25 years.

[7] The Hungarian budgets in recent years have been exceptional in this regard. It is interesting to note that Soviet budgets showed small surpluses in the thirties when inflation was rampant.

[8] See the major study of the Hungarian Scientific Council for World Economy, *Main Tendencies in the World Economy, 1976-1990*, Budapest, 1977, p. 21. According to this report, for the developed capitalist countries, "between 1976-1990, the average growth rate of the GNP will be around 4.5 percent per annum."

[9] Too much emphasis on distribution problems leads to underconsumptionist interpretations of Marx, something that is an anathema for orthodox Marxists. See Michael Bleaney, *Underconsumption Theories: A History and Critical Analysis*, Lawrence and Wishart, 1976.

[10] See my "The Enigma of Soviet Defense Expenditures," *The Journal of Conflict Resolution*," June 1964.

[11] According to the CIA, "estimates of the dollar costs of Soviet defense activities are revised each year to take into account new information and new assessments of the size, composition, and technical characteristics of the Soviet

forces and activities as well as improvements in costing and methodologies . . .
Both Soviet and United States data are updated annually to reflect the most
recent price base possible." See CIA, *A Dollar Comparison of Soviet and
United States Defense Activities, 1967-77*, January 1978, p. 13.

[12] This point is noted by Les Aspin, "The Three Percent Solution; NATO and the
United States Defense Budget," *Challenge*, May-June, 1979, p. 23. According
to the Congressman, "the inadequacy of this measure becomes apparent
when one realizes that if we resumed the draft and reduced pay scales to draft
levels, the Soviet 'dollar' defense budget would plummet substantially because of their abundant manpower."

[13] See the CIA research paper ER79-10131, *Simulations of Soviet Growth Op-
tions to 1985*, March 1979, p. 11, and *The Economist*, "Rearming Without
Tears," August 19, 1978, pp. 9-12. According to the latter editorial, "if Russia
pursued the arms race it has started it may find that a west-in-recession is less
inhibited than it once was about keeping up with it. Higher defense spending is
politically easier than it used to be in the main NATO countries." The editorial concludes: "If the West decides that the balance of power has tipped too
far towards Russia, and that the western rearmament needed to arrest this process is economically feasible and in some ways even economically *desirable*
[my emphasis], Russia could have a problem on its hands."

[14] In this regard, there is an apparent rewriting of history going on. Paul Warnke,
in discussing the partial test ban treaty of 1963 prohibiting atmospheric testing
of nuclear weapons, writes, "As a consequence of *accepting* [my emphasis]
only a limited test ban rather than a comprehensive one, the United States had
to adopt a program that meant greatly accelerated underground testing." The
facts are that the partial test ban treaty was a Soviet concession since they had
been demanding total cessation of tests. As I pointed out at the time, underground testing utilized more resources and was therefore more expensive,
thereby having a diametrically opposite impact on the two economies. Compare Paul Warnke, "Pass the SALT: An Interview with Paul Warnke," *The New
York Review of Books*, June 14, 1979, p. 39, with my letter to the *New York
Times Magazine*, September 8, 1963, VI, p. 16.

Author Index

Subject Index

About the Author

Lynn Turgeon is professor of economics at Hofstra University in Hempstead, New York. During the fall of 1978, he was a Fulbright-Hays lecturer on "Theoretical Problems of American Political Economy" at Moscow State University. This book is based on that series of lectures. Professor Turgeon is the author of *The Contrasting Economies: A Study of Modern Economic Systems*.